Nature Journal
with
John Muir

Nature Journal
with
John Muir

EDITED BY
BONNIE JOHANNA GISEL

I made up a bundle of bread, tied my note-book to my belt, and strode away in the bracing air, full of eager, indefinite hope.

JOHN MUIR

Poetic Matix Press
Madera, CA

Front cover photograph of John Muir and back cover sketch
by John Muir are from the John Muir Papers, Holt-Atherton
Special Collections, University of the Pacific Library.
Copyright 1984 Muir-Hanna Trust.

Cover photograph by Devon Peterson taken in the
Merced River Gorge just outside of Yosemite National Park.

The Resurrection Fern *Polypodium polypodiodies* was collected
by Bonnie Johanna Gisel at Bonaventure Cemetery, Savannah,
Georgia in February 2005 during a trip to study Muir's thousand-mile
walk to the Gulf of Mexico. John Muir placed plants he collected
during his travels between the pages of his journals
to preserve for future study.

Copyright © 2006 by Bonnie Johanna Gisel

First Edition

ISBN 0-9714003-7-7 - hardcover
ISBN 0-9714003-5-0 - paperback

All rights reserved. No part of this book may be used or reproduced
in any manner whatsoever without written permission, except
in the case of quotes for personal use and brief quotations
embodied in critical articles or reviews.

A special thanks to James Downs, and to my family Devon, Kiirsti,
and Laurene for their assistance, and to Bonnie for letting us
get involved in this project. John Peterson, Publisher

Poetic Matrix Press
P.O. Box 1223
Madera, CA 93639
559.673.9402
www.poeticmatrix.com
poeticmatrix@yahoo.com

Nature Journal
with
John Muir

A Nature Journal is a place to grow your thoughts, ideas, observations, and relationship with the natural world. Here on the pages of your journal Natural may flow into you and leave a permanent impression. Out into Nature your words and sketches travel, gathering moss and raindrops, slips of lichen and mountain dust—you are drawn closer to Nature.

John Muir, the inspiration for, and the first president of the Sierra Club, studied and cared about wilderness. He was a poet-naturalist, mountaineer, botanist, and glaciologist. He sought to preserve wild places and is considered one of the founders of the modern environmental movement. Muir was an avid journal keeper. He drew from the many wilderness experiences he recorded in his journals to compose letters to friends, articles, and books through which he shared his sentiments about the natural world and encouraged the preservation of wilderness. Without his journals there would be no letters to family and friends, no articles or books from which we glean an understanding of Muir's relationship with mountains, glaciers, wildflowers, trees, animals, birds, and insects.

This Nature Journal provides an opportunity for you to study the natural world and to grow a deeper relationship with Nature. Through writing and sketching, personal growth and the study of the evolving natural world are literally at your fingertips.

Observing Nature

Nature is the source of inspiration. Observing Nature is equal in importance to writing and sketching in your journal. Look closely at Nature.

Preconceived ideas about the natural world limit your ability to create a union between what you see and what you write and sketch. Clear your mind and be open to discovery.

Look closely at Nature and then look again. Build upon your experience, remember a certain order of events, relate one to another. Remember patterns, motions, and textures. Consider the weather, sky, temperature, and sounds. Reflect upon Nature's temperament.

Select one place that you revisit. Record the changes that occur there season after season.

Carry a field guide to wildflowers, trees, birds, mammals or insects to assist in identification.

How to Begin Writing and Sketching in your Nature Journal

Listen to Nature's voice, literally and figuratively, and provide descriptive words and details for mountains, rivers, streams, flowers, trees, creatures, and the way the natural world interacts and engages in daily and seasonal activity. Consider how you are part of the ecosystem and the diversity around you. Look at Nature as if through a lens. Study sounds, movements, atmosphere.

Incorporate your feelings, moods, observations, and those you might attribute to wildflowers, meadows, rivers, mountains, streams, animals, birds, and insects. Provide Nature with a voice.

Begin writing and sketching. Do not see a blank page as an obstacle, see it as an opportunity! Write and draw often—a few words, a quick sketch. Capture the movement of a lady bug beetle on the edge of your journal or a dragonfly whizzing by. Do not be too critical of your work or edit your writing or erase your drawing to the detriment of spontaneity. Let your observations and ideas flow.

Write as if writing a letter to yourself or to a close friend or family member. Create a narrative, tell a story.

Write prose or poetry or a combination of both. Complete sentences are optional. Complete drawings are optional as well.

Draw pictures with words; incorporate your drawings into your journal and into your sentences. Add photographs or press leaves or wildflowers between the pages.

From the Editor

   Selections from the two-hundred articles written and published by John Muir are offered here to provide stepping-stones for inspiration and thoughtfulness for your writing and sketching journey. Considered to be one of the great mountaineers and one of the earliest plant ecologists, Muir saw with clarity the world he sought to preserve for all time. He was one of Nature's visionaries. As you walk your own pathless journey of discovery in Nature and wilderness may you find that the gentleness of Muir's spirit and the keenness of his sight provide a guiding light as you seek to find ways to draw yourself nearer to the goodness and greatness that abounds upon mountain tops, in warm sunny meadows, and near cool streams.

   Always in Nature.

   Bonnie Johanna Gisel
   LeConte Memorial Lodge
   Yosemite National Park
   2005

NATURE JOURNAL WITH JOHN MUIR

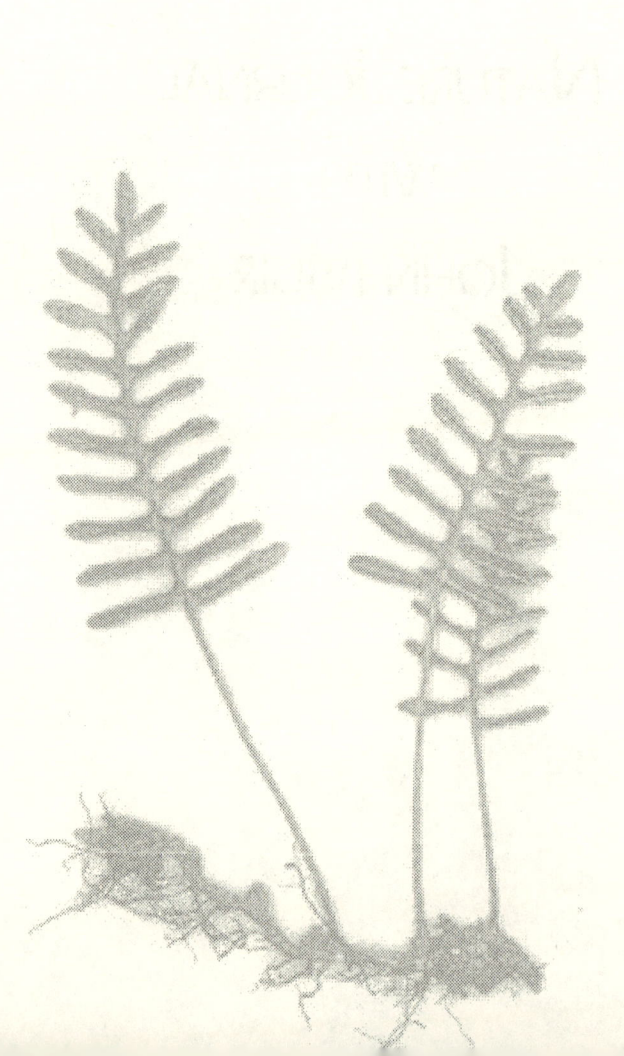

I made up a bundle of bread, tied my note-book to my belt, and strode away in the bracing air, full of eager, indefinite hope.

> The falls respond gloriously to the ripe sunshine of these days. So do the flowers. I have written a song but dare not tell anyone as yet. I never can keep my pen perfectly sober when it gets into the bounce and hurrah of these falls.

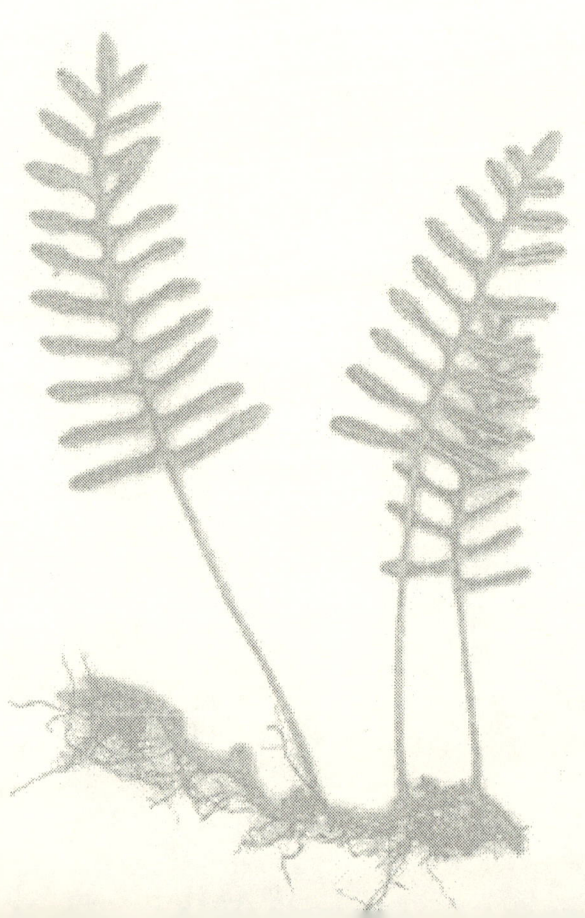

The winds swept along the music curves of many a hill and dale, streaming through the pines, cascading over rocks, and blending all their tones and chords in one grand harmony.

Never were mortal eyes more thronged with beauty. When I walked, more than a hundred flowers touched my feet, at every step closing above them, as if wading in water. Go where I would, east or west, north or south, I still plashed and rippled in flower-gems; and at night I lay between two skies of silver and gold, spanned by a milky-way, and nestling deep in a goldy-way of vegetable suns.

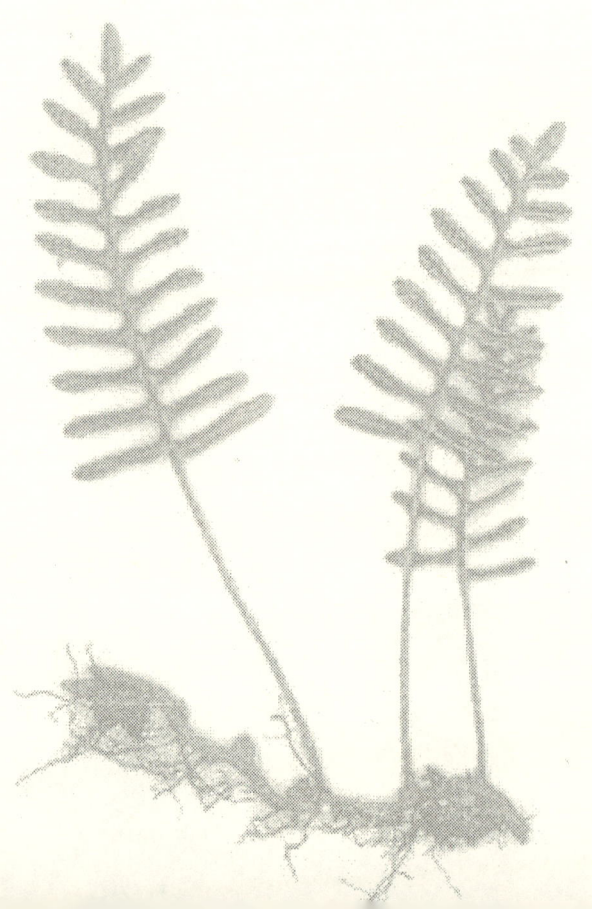

We all travel the milky way together, trees and men; but it never occurred to me until this storm-day, while swinging in the wind, that trees are travelers, in the ordinary sense. They make many journeys, not very extensive ones, it is true; but our own little comes and goes are only little more than tree-wavings.

I began eagerly to sketch the noblest specimens, trying to draw every leaf and branch. This was in 1868. I was perfectly free; and I soon saw that it would be long ere I could get out of those woods, and, as you know, I am not out of them yet.

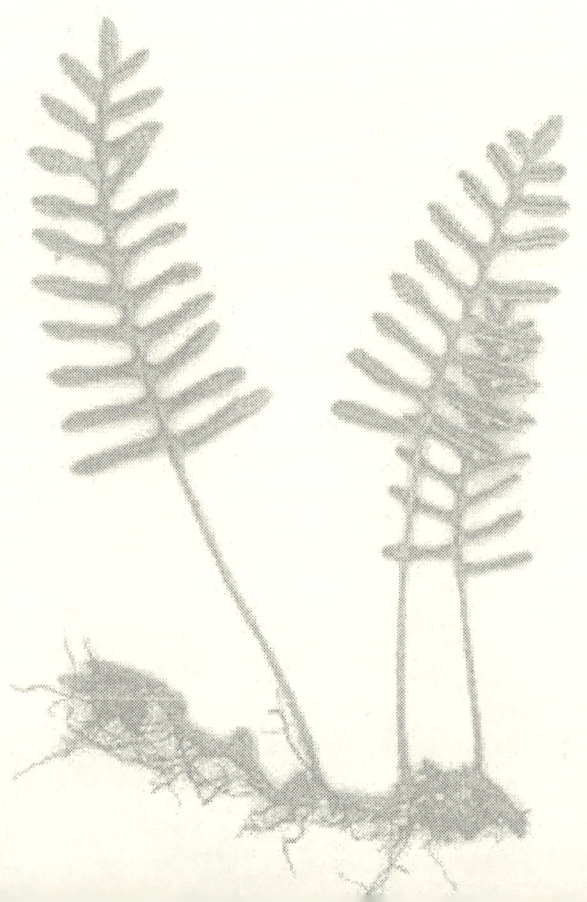

The pine trees shook their tassels dry in the sun, every individual needle tingling and shimmering as if possessed of a separate life. All the mountain voices—birds, winds and leaping, plashing brooks—were tuned to downright gladness.

> Few travelers will, however, take the time to trace out the order or distribution, or the history of the various forests, but no one will weary in admiring special trees.

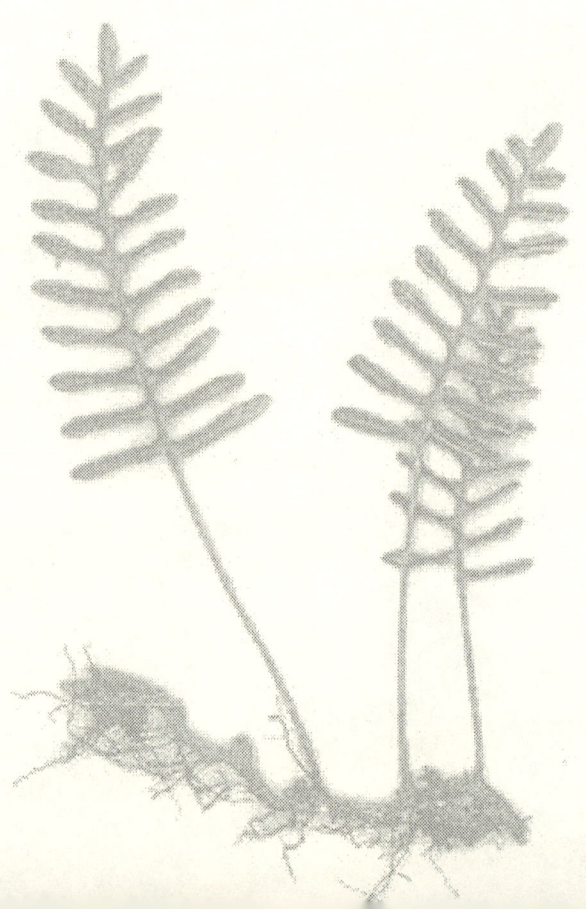

The beauty and completeness of a wild apple-tree living its own life in the woods is heartily acknowledged by all those who have been so happy as to form its acquaintance.

Harmony again becomes visible, and the work of the world goes on as before. The birds feed their young in the trees, the squirrels gather the pinecones around the sides of the valleys, and down on the banks of the cool, gliding rivers the blessed ouzels are singing and dipping confidingly in the shallows, as if saying to every one of these grand manifestations of power round about them, "You also are one of us, each in your place, doing the work appointed you to do ere time began."

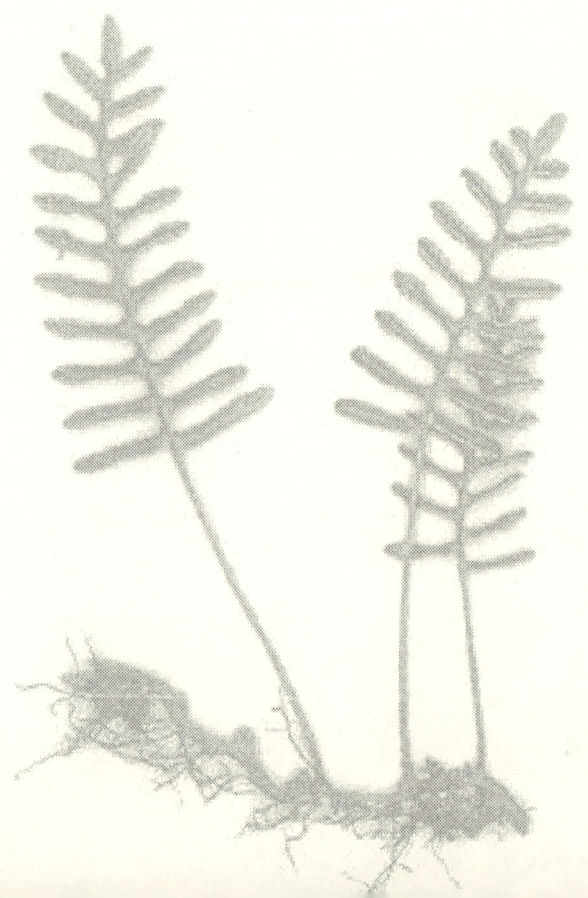

Nature is a good mother, and sees well to the clothing of her many bairns—birds with smoothly imbricated feathers, beetles with shining jackets, and bears with shaggy furs....The squirrel has socks and mittens, and a tail broad enough for a blanket; the grouse is densely feathered down to the ends of his toes; and the wild sheep, besides his under-garment of fine wool, has a thick overcoat of hair that sheds off both the snow and the rain.

With inexpressible delight you wade out into the grassy sun-lake, feeling yourself contained on one of Nature's most sacred chambers, withdrawn from the sterner influences of the mountains, secure from all intrusion, secure from yourself, free in the universal beauty. And notwithstanding the scene is so impressively spiritual, and you seem dissolved in it, yet everything about you is beating with warm, terrestrial human love, delightfully substantial and familiar.

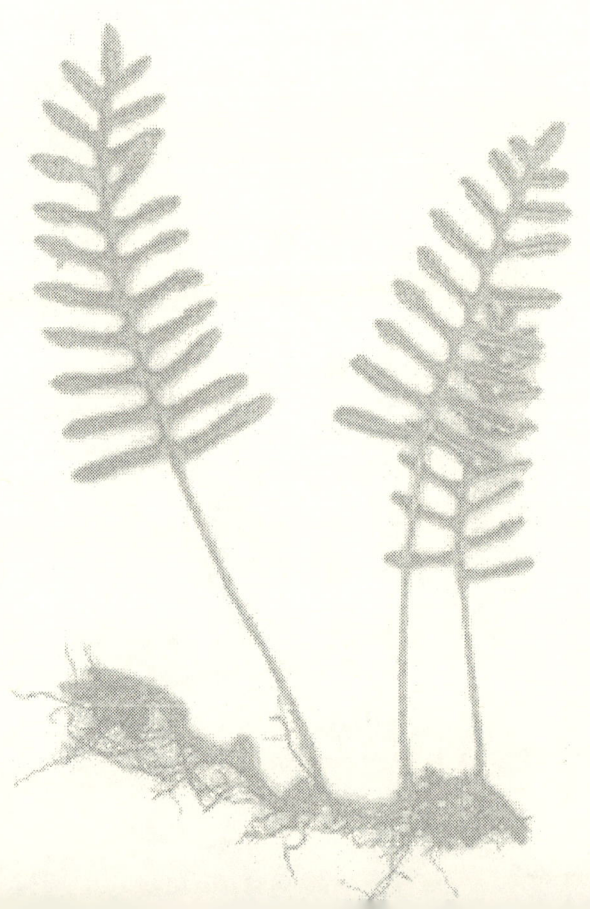

Many a joyful stream is born in the Sierras, but not one can sing like the Merced. In childhood, high on the mountains, her silver thread is a moving melody; of sublime Yosemite she is the voice; the blooming *chaparral* or the flowery plains owe to her fullness their plant-wealth of purple and gold, and to the loose dipping willows and broad green oaks she is bounteous in blessing.

Then came evening, and the somber cliffs were inspired with the ineffable beauty of the alpenglow. A solemn calm fell upon every feature of the landscape. All the lower portion of the canyon was in gloaming shadow, and I crept into a hollow near one of the upper lakelets to smooth away the burrs from a sheltered spot for a bed. When the short twilight faded I kindled a sunny fire, made a cup of tea, and lay down with my face to the deep clean sky. Soon the night-wind began to flow and pour in torrents among the jagged peaks, mingling its strange tones with those of the waterfalls sounding far below.

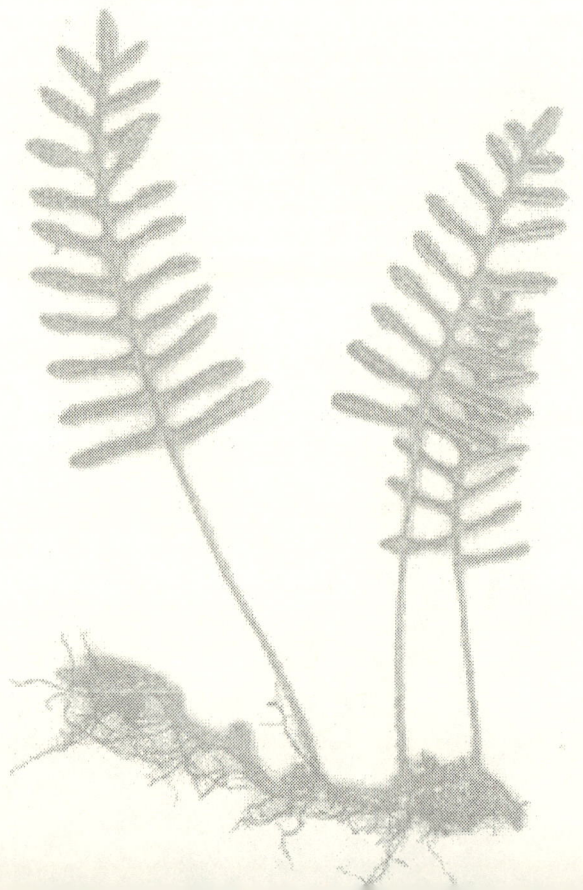

I was awakened in the early morning by the rocking of my cabin and the beating of pine burs on the roof. Detached torrents and avalanches from the main wind-flood overhead were rushing wildly down the narrow side canyons and over the rugged edges of the walls with loud-resounding roar, arousing the giant pines to magnificent activity, and making the entire granite valley throb and tremble like an instrument that was being played.

No cloud in the sky, no storm-tone in the wind. Breakfast of bread and tea was soon made. I fastened a hard, durable crust to my belt by way of provision, in case I should be compelled to pass a night on the mountain-top; then, securing the remainder of my little stock from wolves and wood-rats, I set forth free and hopeful.

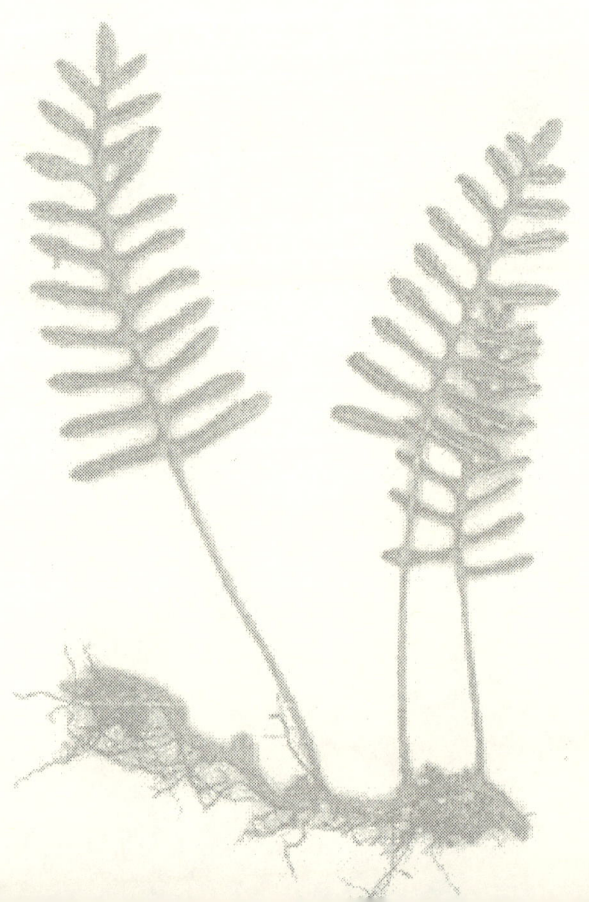

The forests, too, seem kindly familiar, and the lakes and meadows and glad singing streams. I should like to dwell with them forever. Here with bread and water I should be content. Even if not allowed to roam and climb, tethered to a stake or a tree in some meadow or grove, I should be content forever. Bathed in such beauty, watching the expressions ever varying on the faces of the mountains, watching the stars, which here have a glory that the lowlander never dreams of, watching the circling seasons, listening to the songs of the waters and winds and birds, would be endless pleasure. And what glorious cloud-lands I would see, storms and calms, a new heaven and a new earth every day.

I strode on exhilarated, as if never more to feel fatigue, limbs moving of themselves, every sense unfolding like the thawing flowers, to take part in the new day harmony.

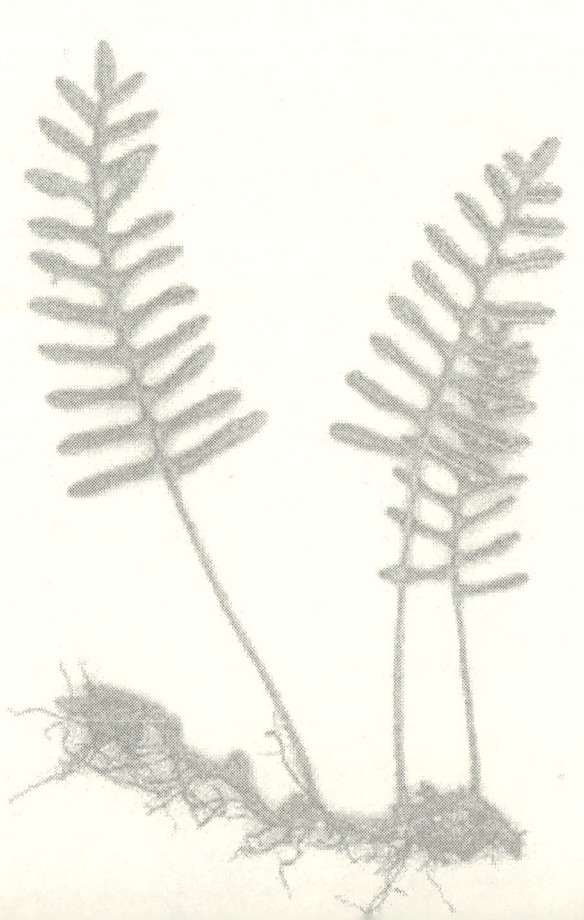

The life of a mountaineer is favorable to the development of soul-life, as well as limb-life, each receiving abundance of exercise and abundance of food.

> A little pure wildness is the one great present want, both of men and sheep.

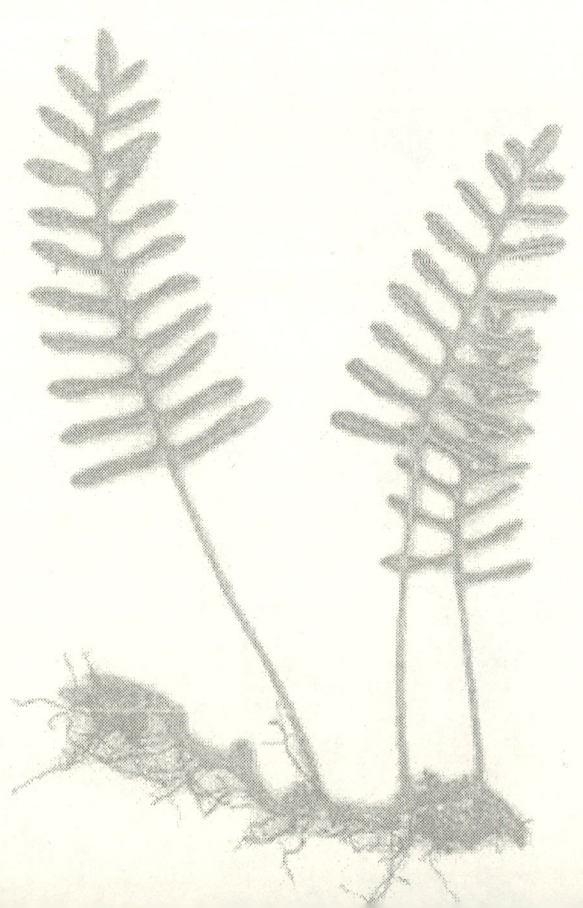

How bright is the shining after summer showers and dewy nights, and after frosty nights in spring and autumn when the morning sunbeams are pouring through the crystals on the bushes and grass, and in winter through the snow-laden trees!

Come all who need rest and light bending and breaking with over work, leave your profits and losses and metallic dividends and come a beeing.

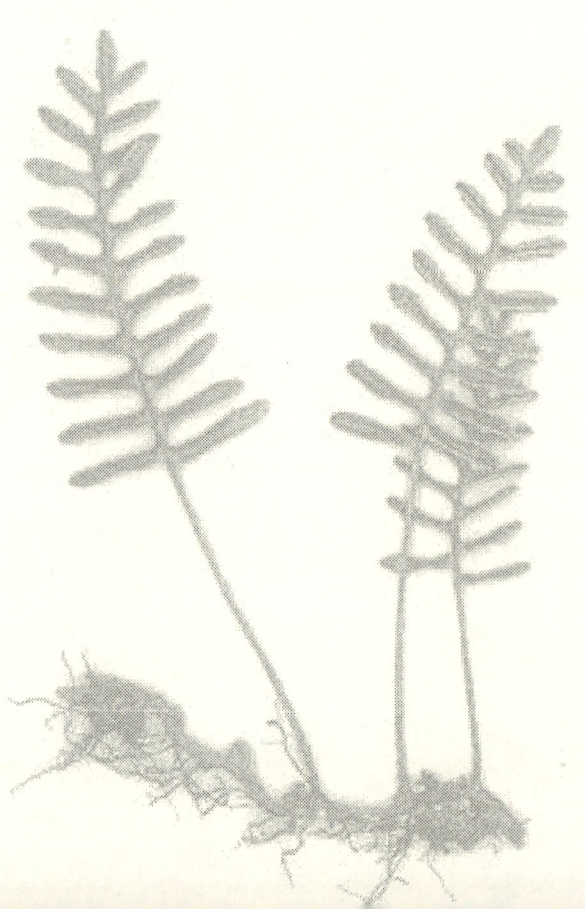

It is impossible to overestimate the value of wild mountains and mountain temples as places for people to grow in, recreation grounds for soul and body.

The walker making the best excursion in pure wilderness. Not necessarily the longest and most dangerous excursion up the highest mountains, through the deepest woods or across the widest torrents, glaciers or deserts, but the one, however, short or long, rough or smooth, calm or stormy, on which the able, fearless walker sees most, learns most, loves most and leaves the cleanest track. Whose heart and mind grow naturally, like trees, gathering inspiration from everything....who learns to regard everything about him as friends and neighbors—the stars, the earth, planets and animals, as well as men.

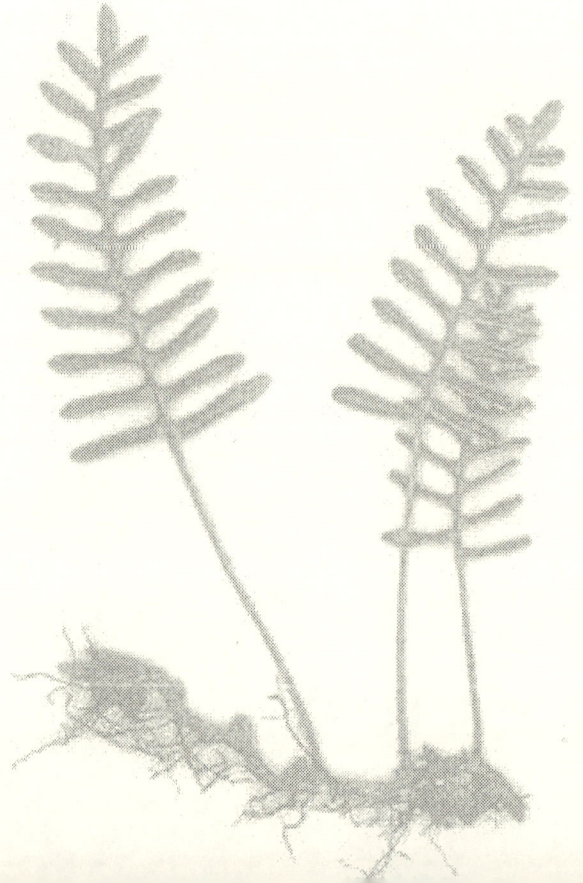

I never before saw a plant so full of life; so perfectly spiritual, it seemed pure enough for the throne of its Creator. I felt as if I were in the presence of superior beings who loved me and beckoned me to come. I sat down beside them and wept for joy. Could angels in their better land show us a more beautiful plant? How good is our Heavenly Father in granting us such friends as are these plant-creatures, filling us wherever we go with pleasure so deep, so pure, so endless.

Only last summer, when I was in the wildest part of the Rocky Mountains, where glaciers still linger and waterfalls like ribbons hang down the unscalable cliffs, I found Linnaea spreading and blooming in glorious exuberance far and wide over mossy ground, beneath spruce and pine,—the wildest and the gentlest, the most beautiful and most loveful of all the inhabitants of the wilderness.

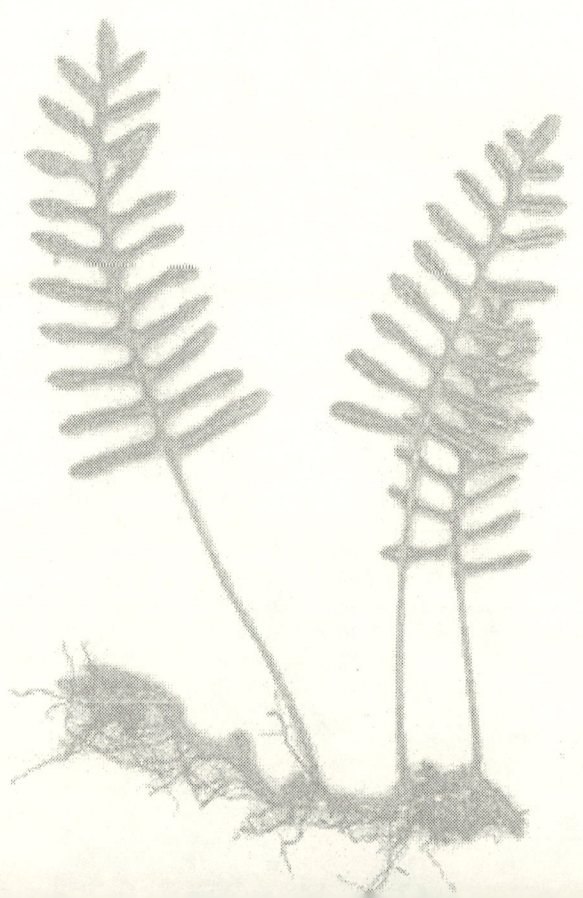

Here, indeed, is the tree-lover's paradise, the woods, dry and wholesome, letting in the light in shimmering masses, half sunshine, half shade, the air indescribably spicy and exhilarating, plushy fir boughs for beds, and cascades to sing us asleep as we gaze through the trees to the stars.

You are all eye, sifted through and through with light and beauty. Sauntering along the brook that meanders silently through the meadow from the east, special flowers call you back to discriminating consciousness.

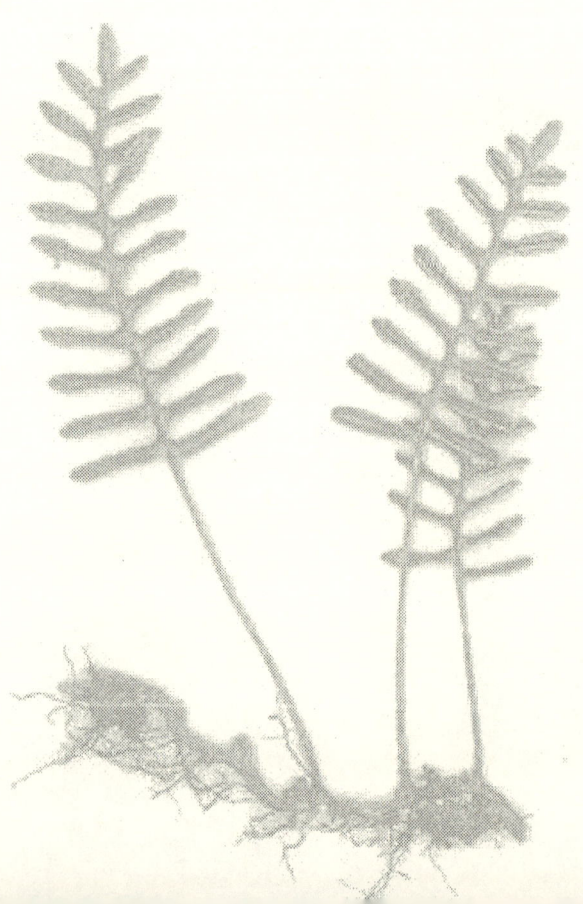

I have often thought in bright, settled sun weather, that I could tell the time of day by the comparative energy of bee movements. Gentle and moderate in the cool of the morning, gradually increasing in fervor, and at high noon thrilling and quivering in wild sun-ecstasy.

After I had bathed in the bright river, sauntered over the meadows, conversed with the domes, and played with the pines, I still felt muddy, and weary, and tainted with the sticky sky of your streets; I determined, therefore, to run out to the higher temples.

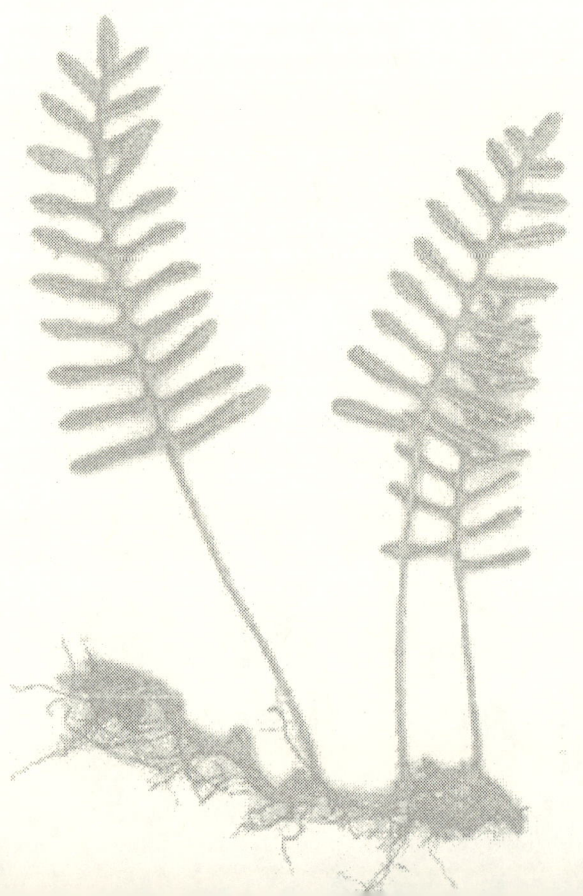

The grand, priest-like pines held their arms above us in blessing; the wind sang songs of welcome; the cool glaciers and the running crystal foundations added their greetings. I was no longer on, but in the mountains: home again, and my pulses were filled. On and on reveling in white moonlight spangles on the streams, shadows in rock hollows and briery ravines, tree architecture on the sky, more divine than ever stars in their spires, leafy mosaic on meadow and bank. Never had the Sierra seemed so inexhaustible. Mile on mile onward in the forest through groves old and young. Pine tassels overarched and brushed both cheeks at once. The chirping of crickets only deepened the stillness.

At length, after attaining an elevation of 12,800 feet, I found myself at the foot of a sheer drop in the bed of the avalanche channel I was tracing, which seemed absolutely to bar all further progress. It is only about forty-five or fifty feet high, and somewhat roughened by fissures and projections; but these seemed so slight and insecure, as footholds, that I tried hard to avoid the precipice altogether, by scaling the wall on either side. But, though less steep, the walls were smoother than the obstructing rock, and repeated efforts only showed that I must either go right ahead or turn back. The tried dangers beneath seemed even greater than that of the cliff in front; therefore, after scanning its face again and again, I commenced to scale it, picking my holds withintense caution. After gaining a point about half-way to the top, I was brought to a dead stop, with arms outspread, clinging close to the face of the rock, unable to move hand or foot either up or down. My doom appeared fixed. I must fall.

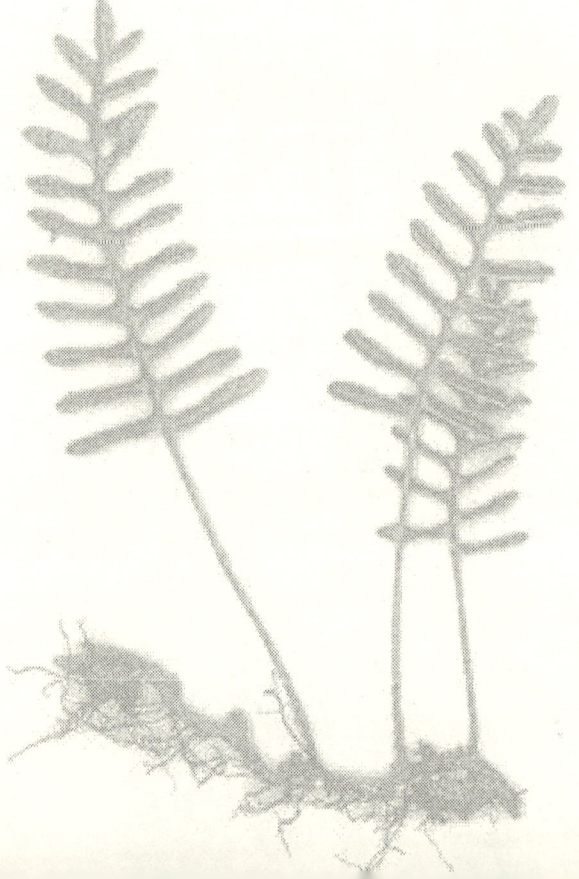

When this final danger flashed in upon me, I became nerve-shaken for the first time since setting foot on the mountain, and my mind seemed to fill with a stifling smoke. This terrible eclipse lasted only a moment, when life blazed forth again with preternatural clearness. I seemed suddenly to become possessed of a new sense. The other self—the ghost of by-gone experiences, Instinct, or Guardian Angel—call it what you will—came forward and assumed control. Then my trembling muscles became firm again, every rift and flaw in the rock was seen as through a microscope, and my limbs moved with a positiveness and precision with which I seemed to have nothing at all to do. Had I been borne aloft upon wings, my deliverance could not have been more complete.

It is after both the body and soul of a mountaineer have worked hard, and enjoyed much, that they are most palpably separate. Our weary limbs, lying restingly among the pine-needles, make no attempt to follow after or sympathize with the nimble spirit, that, apparently glad of the opportunity, runs off along the beetling cliffs, or away among the peaks and glaciers of the farthest landscapes, or into realms that eye hath not seen, nor ear heard.

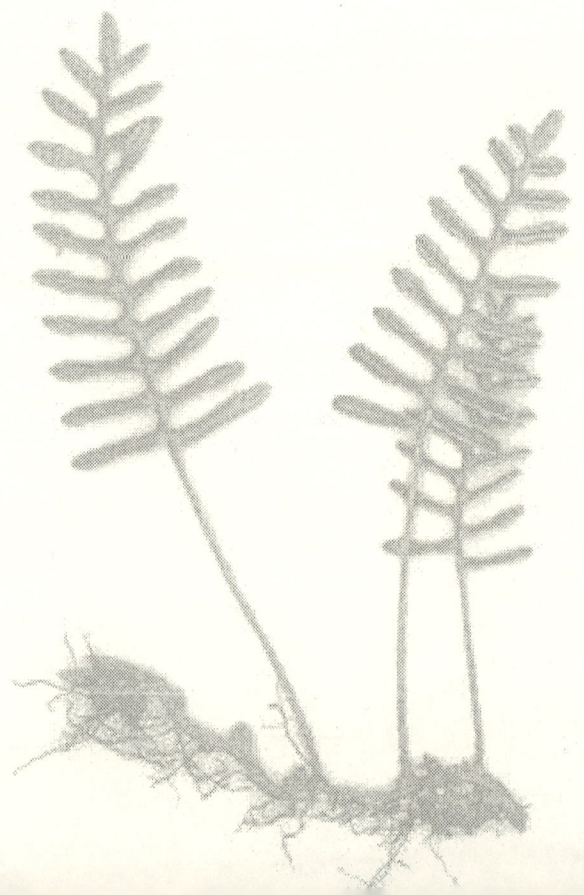

Men ascend mountains as instinctively as squirrels ascend trees, and, of course, the climbing of Mount Whitney was a capital indulgence, apart from the enjoyment drawn from landscapes and scientific pursuits.

Early in the forenoon the clouds lifted and the sun shone out, revealing a host of noble mountains, grandly sculptured and composed, and robed in spotless white, some of the highest adorned with streamers of mealy snow wavering in the wind—a truly glorious spectacle.

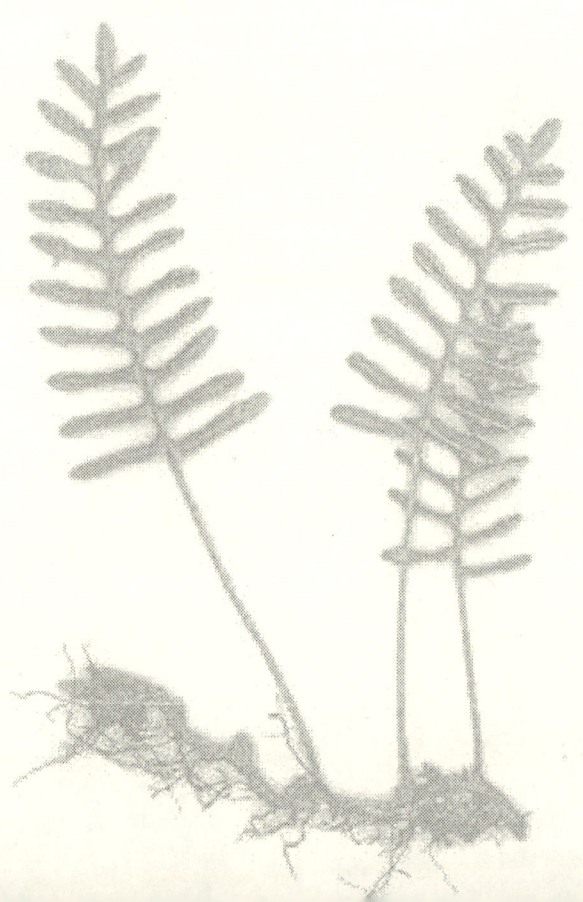

How memorable are these Sierra experiences! Describing one day from the depths of the upper forest we rambled enchanted through the sugar-pine groves of Deer Park. Never did pines seem more noble and devout in all their gestures and tones. The sun, pouring down floods of mellow light, seemed to be thinking only of them, and the wind gave them voice; but the gestures of their outstretched arms seemed independent of the wind, and impressed us with solemn awe as if we were strangers in a new world.

Happy is the man with the will and the time to climb a silver fir in full flower and fruit. How admirable the forest work of Nature is seen to be as one ascends from branch to branch, all arranged in regular collars around the trunk, one above the other like the whorled leaves of lilies, and with each branch and branchlet about as strictly pinnate as the most exact and symmetrical fern frond.

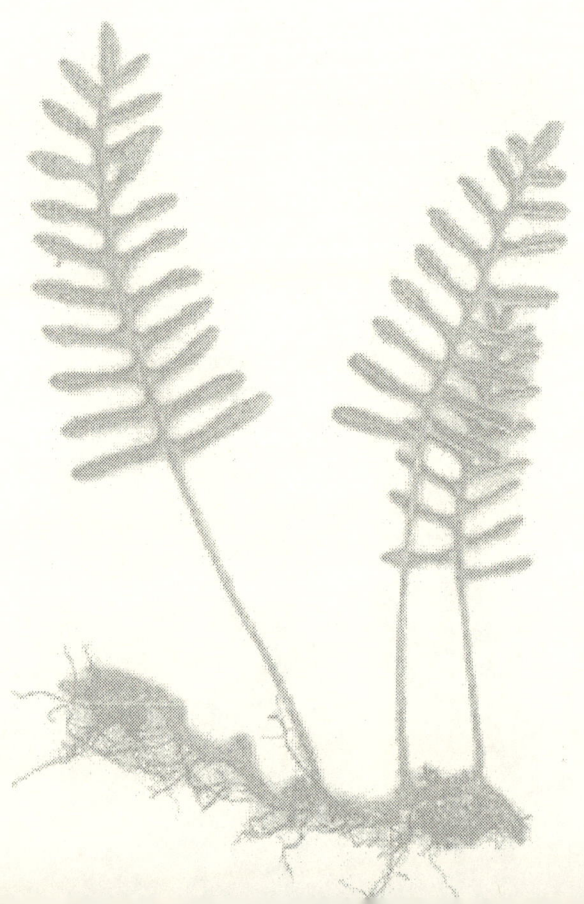

Healthy mountaineers always discover in themselves a reserve of power after great exhaustion.

The forests of America, however slighted by man, must have been a great delight to God; for they were the best he ever planted. The whole continent was a garden, and from the beginning it seemed to be favored above all the other wild parks and gardens of the globe.

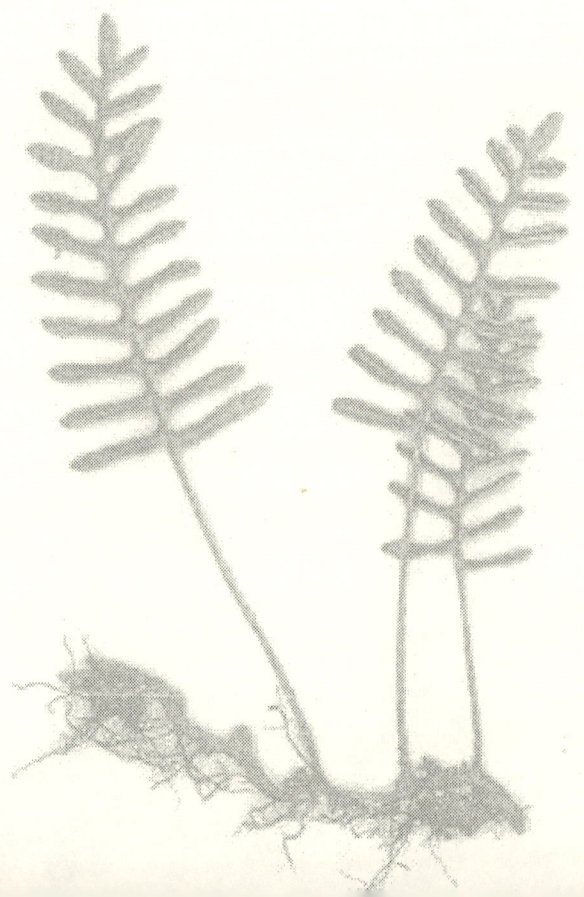

Any fool can destroy trees. They cannot run away; and if they could, they would still be destroyed—chased and hunted down as long as fun or a dollar could be got out of their bark hides, branching horns, or magnificent bole backbones. Few that fell trees plant them; nor would planting avail much towards getting back anything like the noble primeval forests. During a man's life only saplings can be grown, in the place of the old trees—tens of centuries old—that have been destroyed. It took more than three thousand years to make some of the trees in these Western woods—trees that are still standing in perfect strength and beauty, waving and singing in the mighty forests of the Sierra. Through all the wonderful, eventful centuries since Christ's time—and long before that—God has cared for these trees, saved them from drought, disease, avalanches, and a thousand straining, leveling tempests and floods; but he cannot save them from fools—only Uncle Sam can do that.

The granite domes and pavement, apparently imperishable, we take as symbols of permanence, while these crumbling peaks, down whose frosty gullies avalanches are ever falling, are symbols of change and decay. Yet all alike, fast or slow, are surely vanishing away. Nature is ever at work building and pulling down, creating and destroying, keeping everything whirling and flowing, allowing no rest, but in rhythmical motion, chasing everything in endless song out of one beautiful form into another.

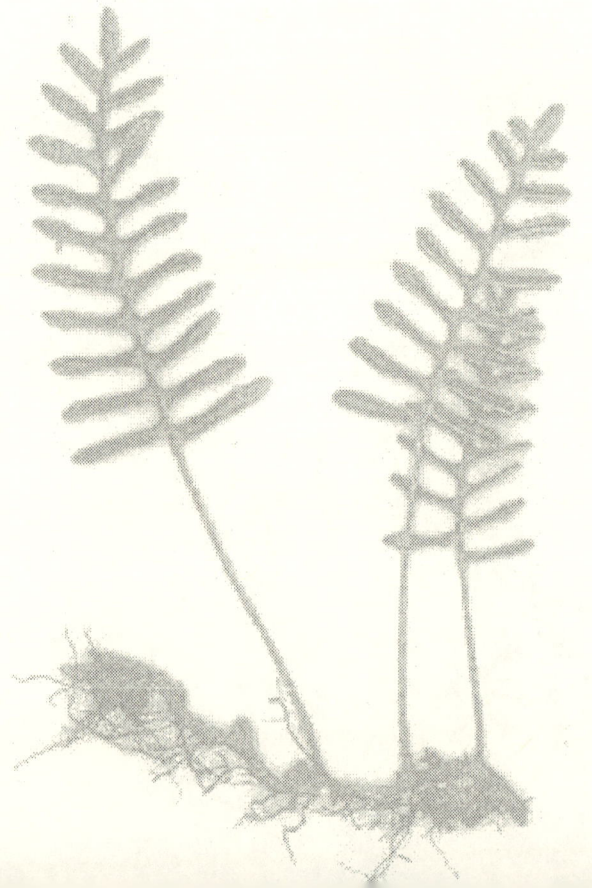

I sauntered down through the dripping bushes, reveling in the universal vigor and freshness with which all the life about me was inspired. The woods were born again. How clean and unworn, and immortal the world seemed to be!

The empty clouds changed to purple and pure snowy white, shot through and through with the sun, and the dripping trees were laden with flashing, irised crystals that burned on every leaf. The clouds moved hither and thither, now down among the canyon rocks, now up among the rejoicing forests, as if reviewing their accomplished work.

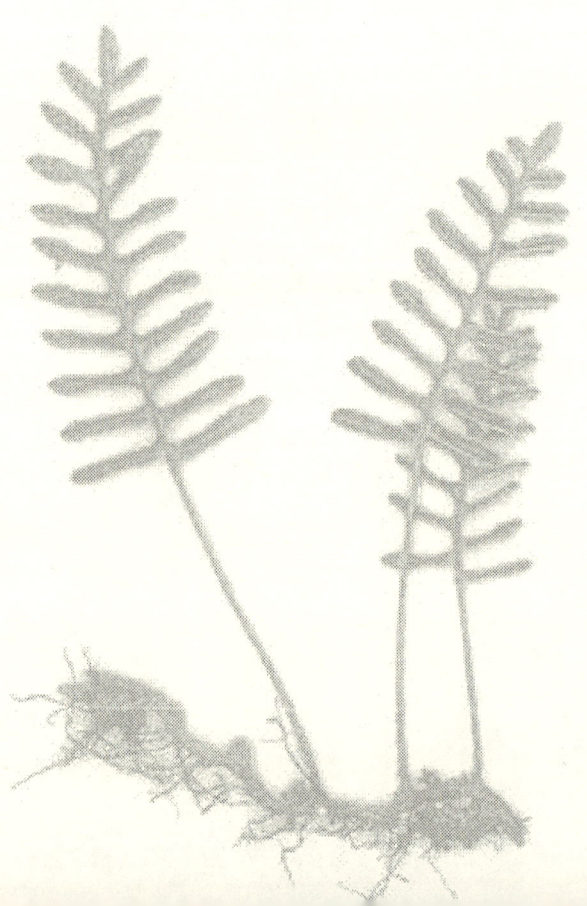

The birds were gathered beneath leafy shadows, or made short, languid flights in search of food. All, save the majestic buzzard; with broad wings outspread, he sailed the warm ether unweariedly from ridge to ridge, seeming to enjoy the fervid sun glow like a butterfly.

> Plant-color fills the valley in light floating clouds and mists;
> it covers the ground and trees, and chaparral and tabled rocks,
> coming in small flakes from the impartial snow.

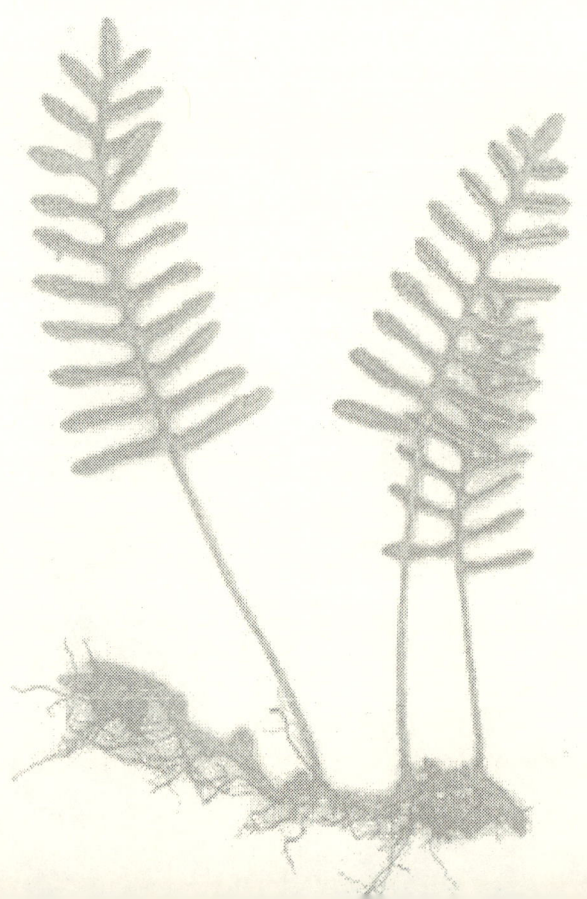

Many bold insects go mountaineering almost as soon as they are born, ascending the highest summits on the mild breezes that blow in from the sea every day during steady weather; but comparatively few of these adventurers find their way down or see a flower bed again. Getting tired and chilly, they alight on the snow fields and glaciers, attracted perhaps by the glare, take cold, and die.

Few nights of my mountain life have been more eventful than that of my ride in the woods from Coulterville, when I made my reunion with the winds and pines. It was eleven o'clock when we reached Black's ranch. I was weary, and soon died in sleep. How cool, and vital, and re-creative was the hale young mountain air! On, higher, higher, up into the holy of holies of the woods. Pure, white, lustrous clouds overshadowed the massive congregations of silver fir and pine. We entered, and a thousad living arms were waved in solemn blessing. An infinity of mountain life. How complete is the absorption of one's life into the spirit of mountain woods!

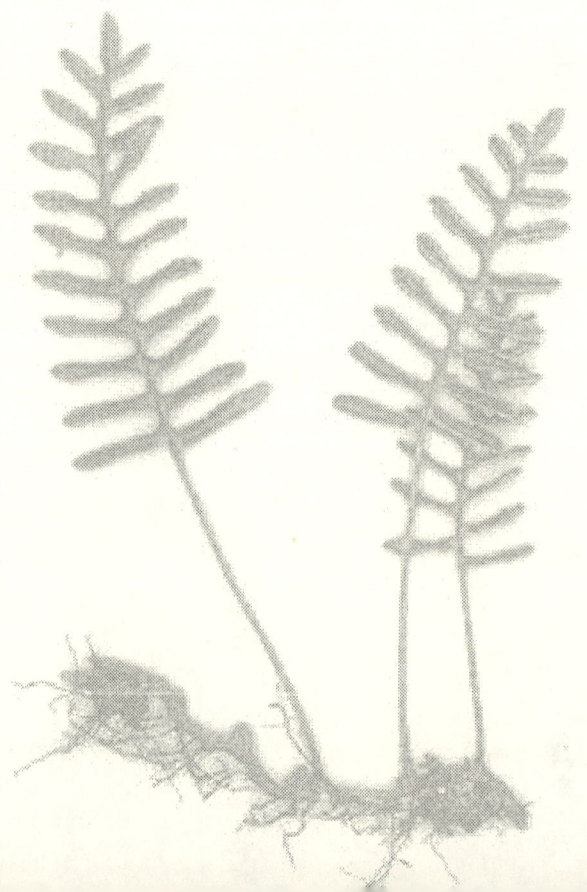

The dawn, as in all the pure, dry desert country, is ineffably beautiful; and when the first level sunbeams sting the domes and spires, with what a burst of power the big, wild days begin! The dead and the living, rocks and hearts alike, awake and sing the new-old song of creation....Every rock temple then becomes a temple of music; every spire and pinnacle an angel of light and song, shouting color halleluiahs.

There are not deserts, as we understand them. Nature's love is universal, and in no other place have I heard this doctrine proclaimed in plainer terms than in the storm-beaten solitudes of the Mono Pass.

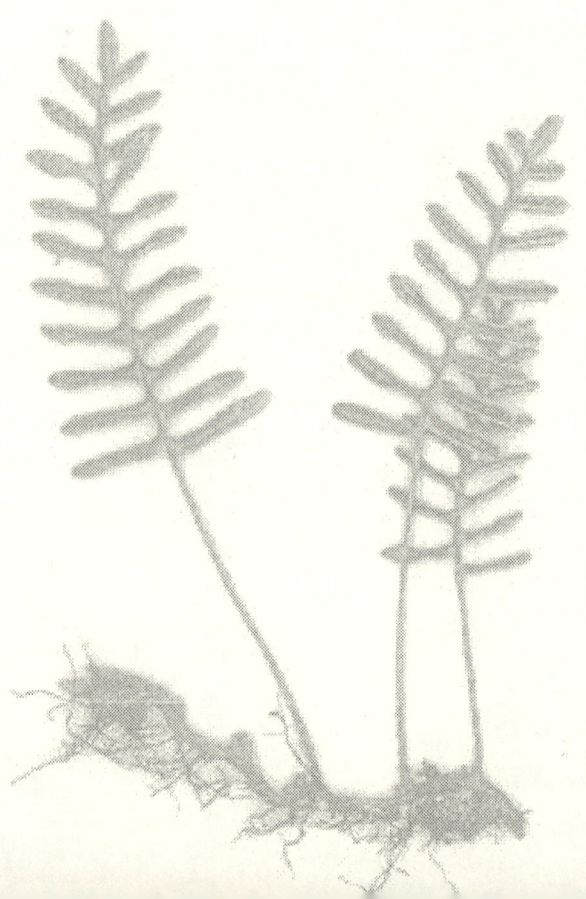

Standing here, with facts so fresh and telling and held up so vividly before us, every seeing observer, not to say geologist, must readily apprehend the earth-sculpturing, landscape-making action of flowing ice. And here, too, one easily learns that the world, though made, is yet being made. That this is still the morning of creation. That mountains long conceived, are now being born, brought to light by the glaciers, channels traced for rivers, basins hollowed for lakes. That moraine soil is being ground and outspread for coming plants—coarse boulders and gravel for the forests—finer meal for grasses and flowers—while the finest, water-bolted portion of the grist, seen hastening far out to sea, is being stored away in the darkness, and builded, particle on particle, cementing and crystallizing, to make the mountains and valleys and plains of other landscapes, which, like fluent, pulsing water, rise and fall, and pass on through the ages in endless rhythm and beauty.

Perhaps you have already said that you have seen enough for a lifetime. But before you go away you should spend at least one day and a night on a mountain top, for a last general calming, settling view.

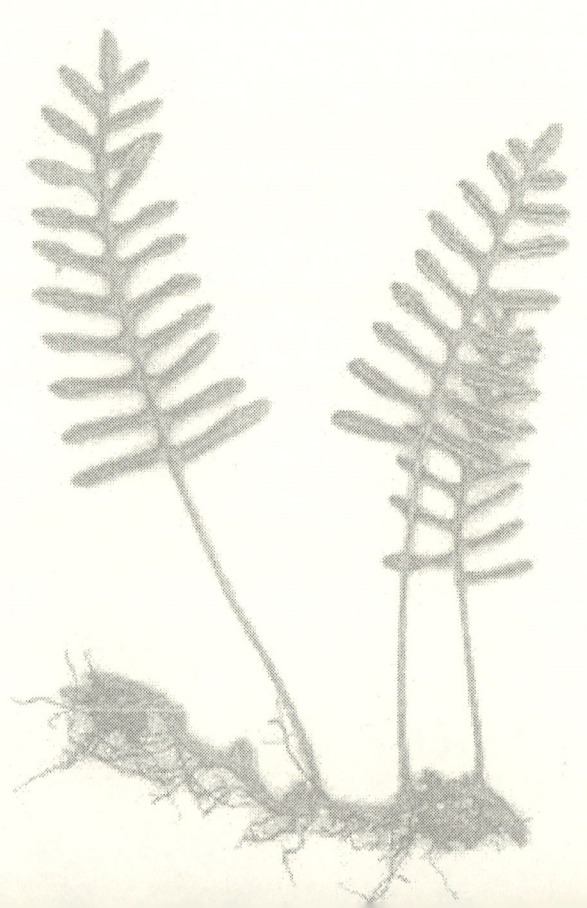

The sky was of the thinnest, purest azure; spiritual life filled every
pore of rock and cloud; and we reveled in the marvelous
abundance and beauty of the landscapes by which
we were encircled.

I started up the Canyon of Tenaya, caring little about the quantity of bread I carried; for, I thought, a fast and a storm and a difficult canyon are just the medicine I require.

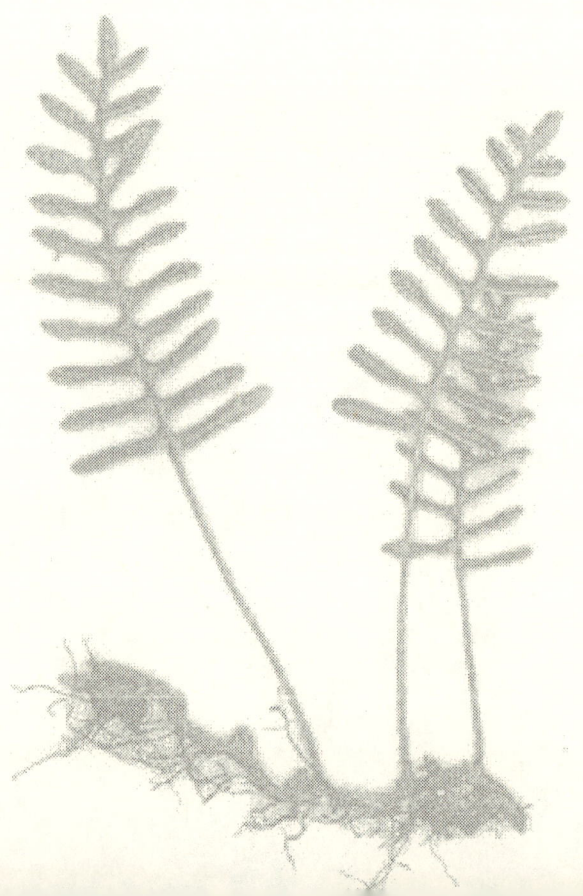

Descending the divide in a hesitating mood, I picked my way across the yawning chasm at the foot, and climbed out upon the glacier. There were no meadows now to cheer with their brave colors, nor could I hear the dun-headed sparrows, whose cherry notes so often relieve the silence of our highest Alps. The gurgling of small rills down the veins and crevasses, and ever and anon the rattling report of failing stones, with the echoes they shot out into the crisp air,—these were the only sounds.

I escaped from the gorge about noon, after accomplishing some
of the most delicate feats of mountaineering I ever attempted;
and here the canyon is all broadly open again—a dead lake,
luxuriantly forested with pine, and spruce, and silver fir,
and brown-trunked *Libocedrus*.

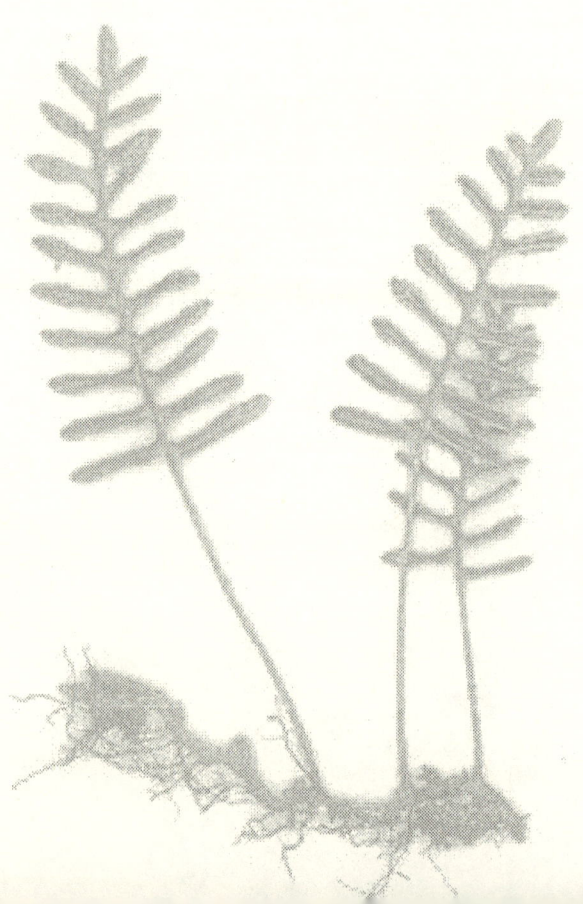

I met Cassiope, growing in fringes among the battered rocks. Her blossoms had faded long ago, but they were still clinging with happy memories to the evergreen sprays, and still so beautiful as to thrill every fiber of one's being. Winter and summer, you may hear her voice, the low, sweet melody of her purple bells. No evangel among all the mountain plants speaks Nature's love more plainly than Cassiope. Where she dwells, the redemption of the coldest solitude is complete. The very rocks and glaciers seem to feel her presence, and become imbued with her own fountain sweetness.

Nature is ever at work building and pulling down, creating and destroying, keeping everything whirling and flowing, allowing no rest but in rhythmical motion, chasing everything in endless song out of one beautiful form into another.

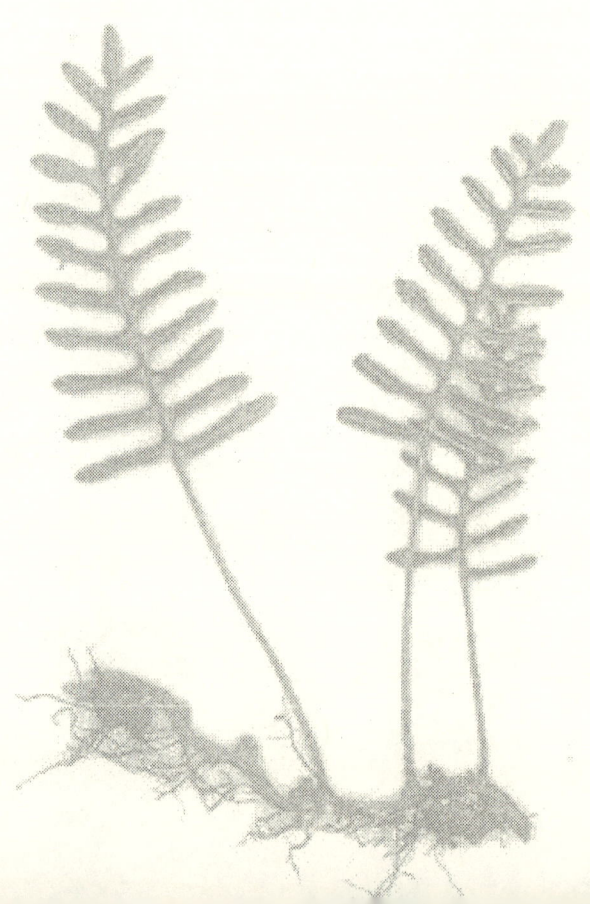

We are governed more than we know, and most when we are wildest. Plants, animals, and stars are all kept in place, bridled along appointed ways, with one another, and through the midst of one another—killing and being killed, eating and being eaten, in harmonious proportions and quantities.

> No matter what may be the note which any creature forms in the song of existence, it is made first for itself, then more and more remotely for all the world and worlds.

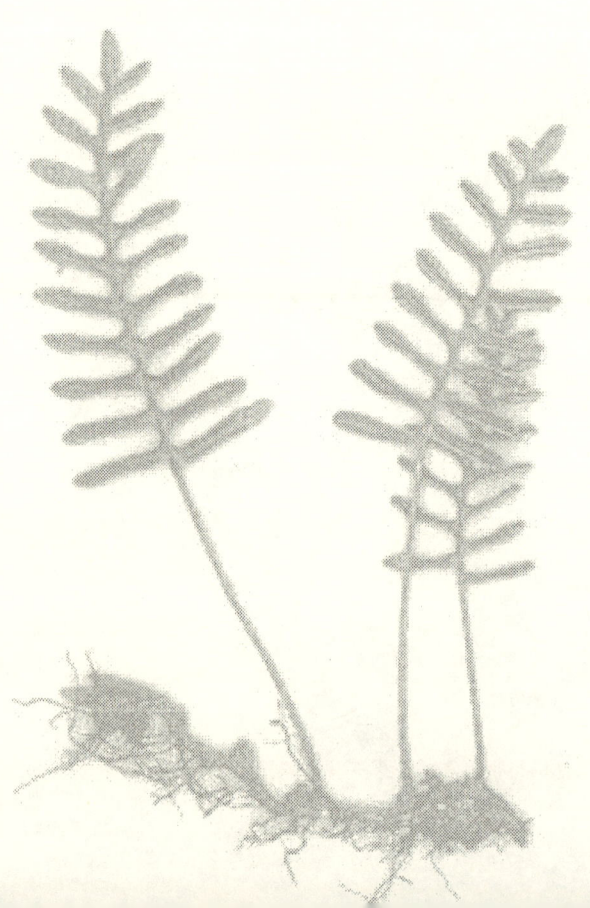

All the wilderness is medicine....With a little tea and sugar, take plenty of flour, beans, rice, dried fruit and warm clothing; and forget and leave behind as much of everything else as you can. Be thoughtful about your feet. Try to bathe them three or four times a day, and clothe them with the utmost care. Loose-fitting, thick and perfectly dry footwear is required. Few know what 50 degrees below zero means to the toes. Of course you will learn, but your frost lessons may be costly.

It was not long, however, before I discovered a crooked seam in the rock, by which I was enabled to climb to the edge of a terrace that crosses the canyon, and divides the cataract nearly in the middle. Here I sat down to take breath and make some entries in my notebook, taking advantage, at the same time, of my elevated position above the trees to gaze back over the valley into the heart of the noble landscape, little knowing the while what neighbors were near. After spending a few irregular minutes in this way, I chanced to look across the fall, and there stood three sheep quietly observing me.

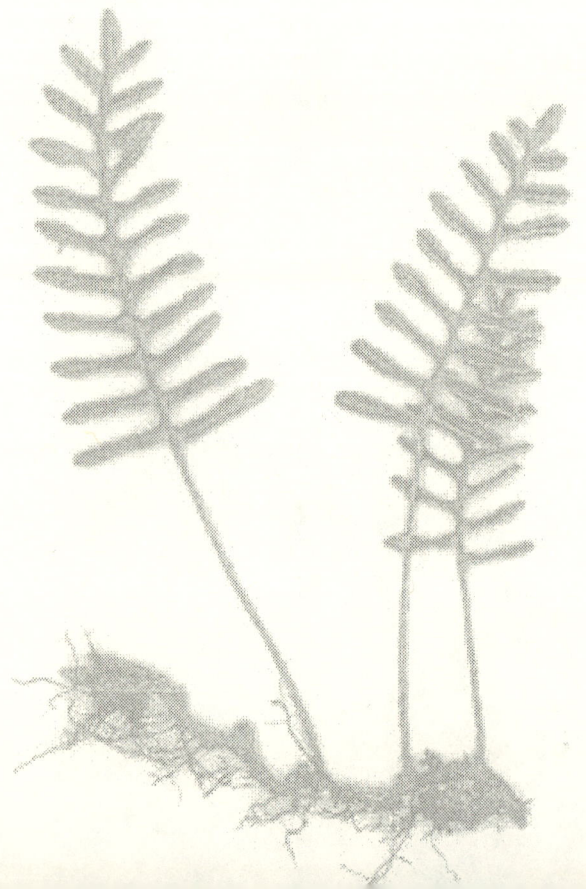

Pushing on up the rugged slopes, I found many delightful seclusions—moist nooks at the foot of cliffs, and lilies in every one of them, not growing close together like daisies, but well apart, with plenty of room for their bells to swing free and ring.

Good bread on which your climbing and digging depends, may be made direct from the flour-sack, with a little salt and water stirred in. After the dough is worked to the required firmness squeeze it into thin cakes about the size of ship biscuits, throw them on hot coals raked from the heart of your camp fire, turn them before they begin to burn, and when firm enough set them on edge to be toasted until thoroughly baked through.

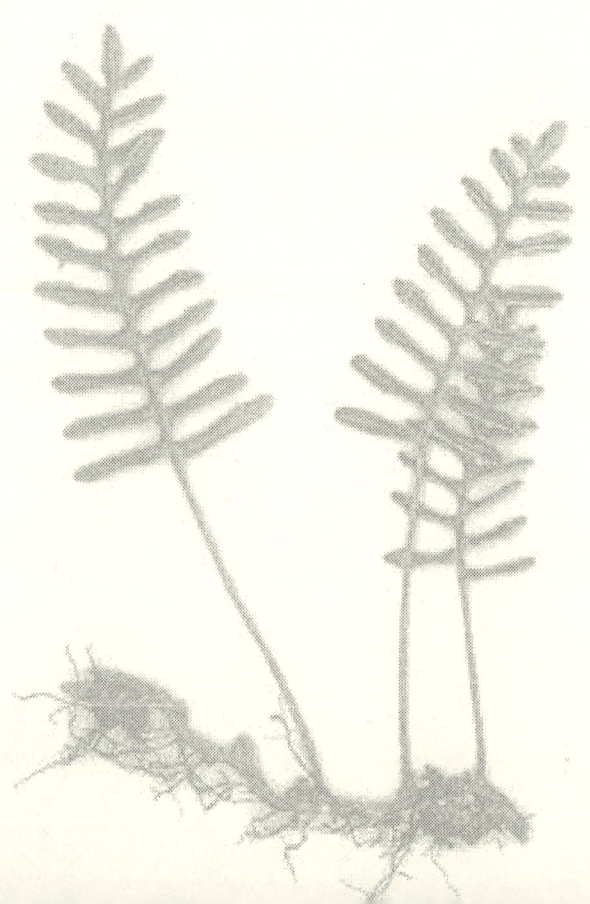

If the weather is bad, or you are camped in a boggy place, cut a stick about the size of a whip-handle, of birch, pine, spruce, cottonwood or willow, according to the flavor desired, and sharpen it, squeeze out a handful of dough, coil it in a thin spiral around the stick and set it upright in the ground at baking distance from the fire, giving it a quarter turn from time to time until the bread spiral is thoroughly baked and browned all around.

As the day draws to a close, shadows, wondrous, black, and thick, like those of the morning, fill up the wall hollows, while the glowing rocks, their rough angles burned off, seem soft and hot to the heart as they stand submerged in purple haze, which now fills the canyon like a sea. Still deeper, richer, more divine grow the great walls and temples, until in the supreme flaming glory of sunset the whole canyon is transfigured, as if all the life and light of centuries of sunshine stored up and condensed in the rocks was now being poured forth as from one glorious fountain, flooding both earth and sky.

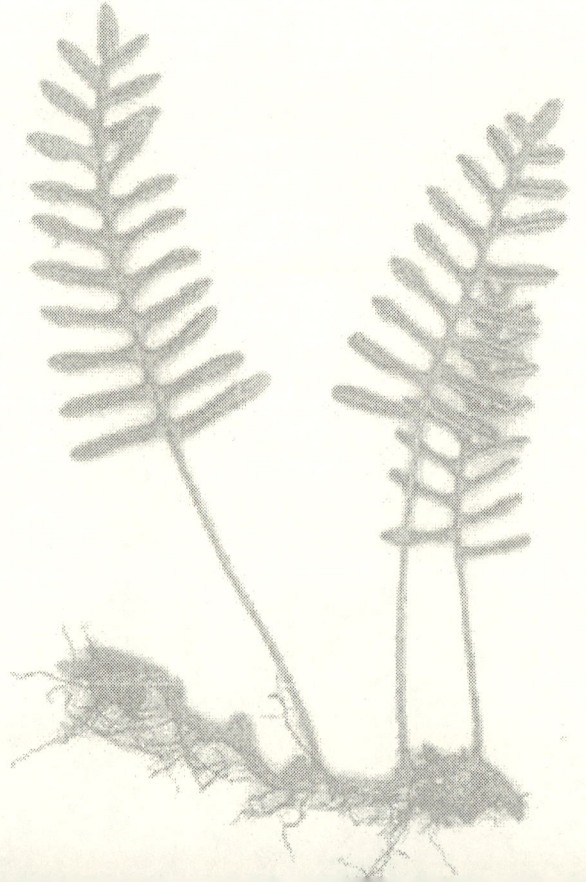

How beautiful is the fire-light on the nearest larkspurs
and geraniums and daisies of our gardens! How hearty the
wave-greeting on the rocks below, sent us by the two glaciers!
And how glorious a song the sixteen cascades are singing!

I made my bed in a nook of a pine-thicket, where the branches were pressed and crinkled overhead like a roof, and bent down around the sides. These are the best bed-chambers our Alps afford—snug as squirrel-nests, well ventilated, full of spicy odors, and with plenty of wind-played needles to sing one asleep. I little expected company, but, creeping in through a low side door, I found five or six birds nestling among the tassels. The night-wind began to blow soon after dark; at first, only a gentle breathing, but increasing toward midnight to a violent gale that fell upon my leafy roof in ragged surges, like a cascade, and bearing strange sounds from the crags overhead. The water-fall sang in chorus, filling the old ice-fountain with its solemn roar, and seeming to increase in power as the night advanced....I had to creep out many times to the fire during the night; for it was biting cold and I had no blankets. Gladly I welcomed the morning star.

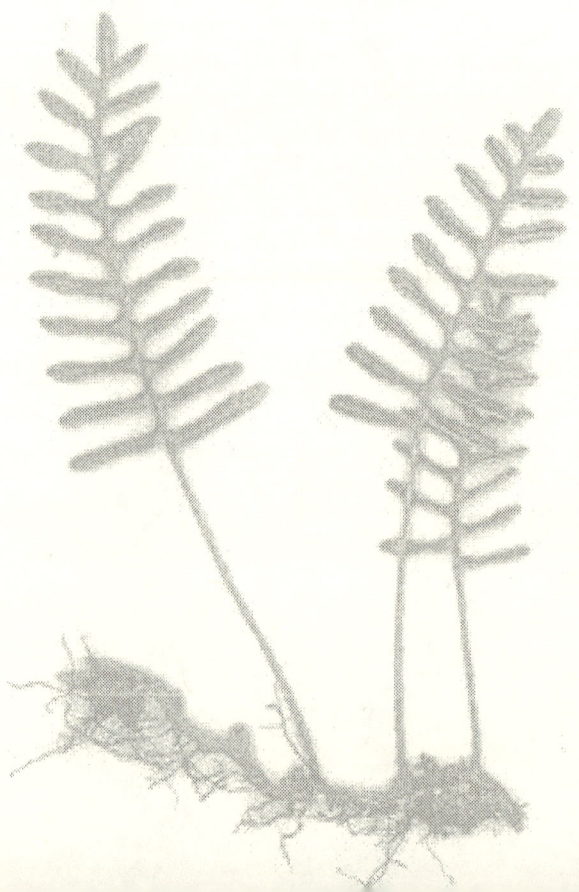

The slant yellow sunshine was streaming over the islands, silvering the mirror water, and lighting a widening swath of flashing, shimmering spangles along the rippled wake of our boat. The natural love of wild beauty that forms an essential part of every human being began to declare itself. Every eye was beaming and appreciative. Gaze in any direction, forward, back on either hand, soul and sight were filled.

How strange seem these untamed solitudes of the wild free bosom of the Alaska woods. Nevertheless they are found necessarily and eternally familiar. Go where we will, all over the world, we seem to have been there before.

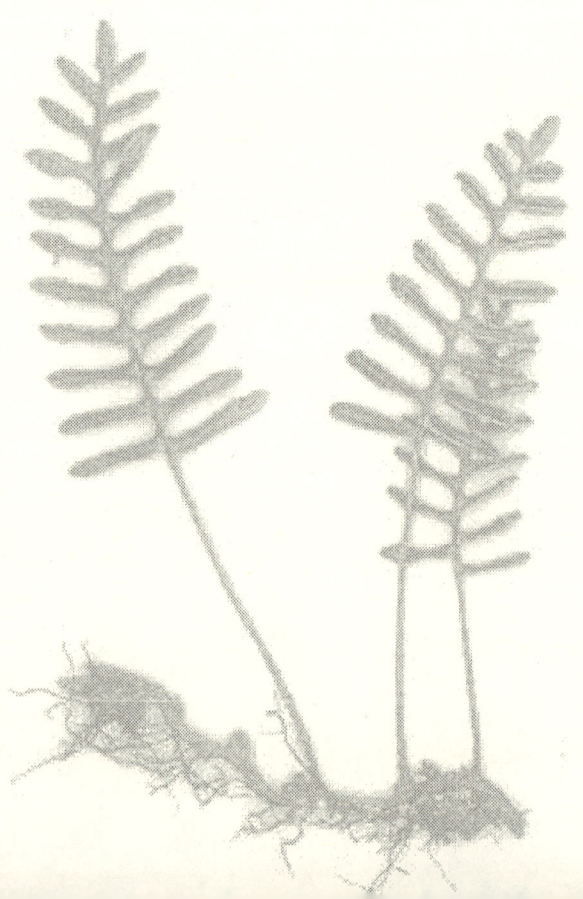

Returning to the canoe, we pushed off, and in a few moments were racing over the bar with lightning speed through leaping waves, and swirling eddies, and sheets of rock-dashed foam; our little shell of a boat tossed and twirled as lightly as a bubble. Then rowing across a belt of back-flowing water, we found ourselves gliding calmly along a smooth mirror reach between granite walls of the very wildness and most exciting description conceivable.

The winds were hushed, the tundra glowed in creamy golden sunshine, and the colors of the ripe foliage of the hearthworts, willows, and birch—red, purple, and yellow, in pure bright tones— were enriched with those of berries which were scattered everywhere, as if they had been showered from the clouds like hail.

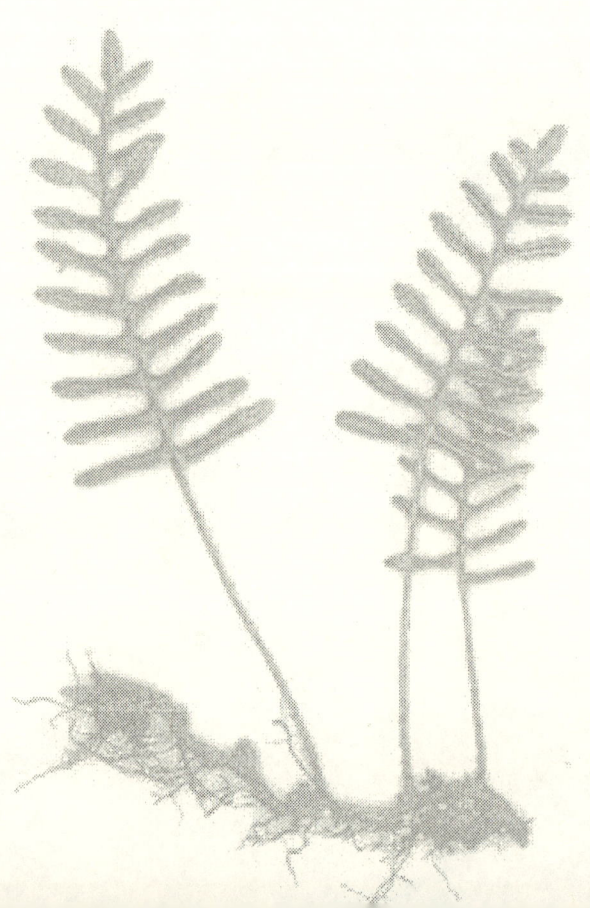

Winds are advertisements of all they touch, however much or little we may be able to read them; telling their wanderings even by their scents alone.

> Gliding on and on, the scenery seemed at every turn to become more lavishly fruitful in forms as well as more sublime in dimensions. Snowy falls booming in splendid dress, colossal domes, and battlements, and sculptured arches of a fine neutral gray tint, all laved by the deep blue water; green ferny dells, bits of flower bloom on ledges, fringes of willow and birch, and glaciers above all.

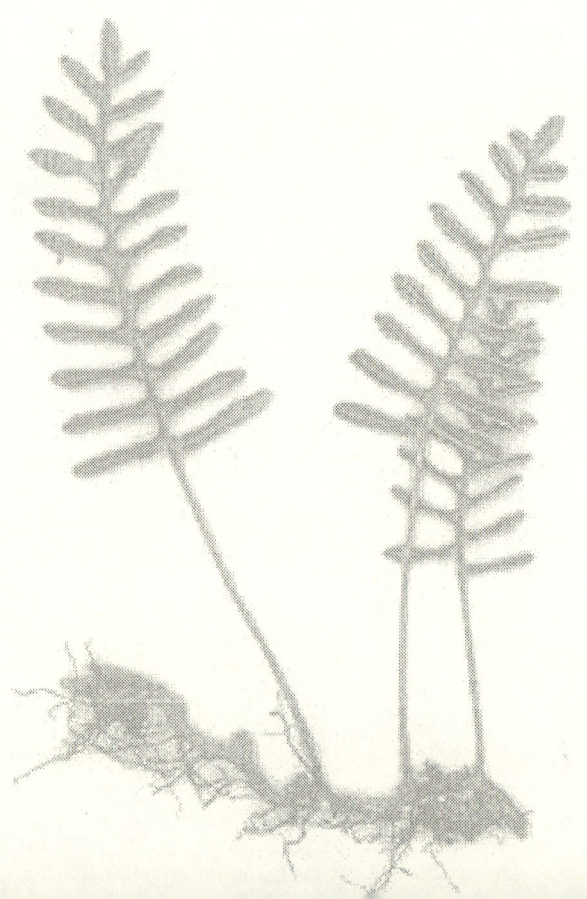

The disbanding clouds lingered lovingly about the mountains, filling the canyons like tinted wool, rising and drooping around the topmost peaks, fondling their rugged bases, or, sailing alongside, trailed their lustrous fringes through the pines as if taking a last view of their accomplished work. Then came darkness, and the glorious day and the storm were done.

> To the sane and free it will hardly seem necessary to cross the continent in search of wild beauty, however easy the way, for they find it in abundance wherever they chance to be. Like Thoreau they see forests in orchards and patches of huckleberry brush, and oceans in ponds and drops of dew.

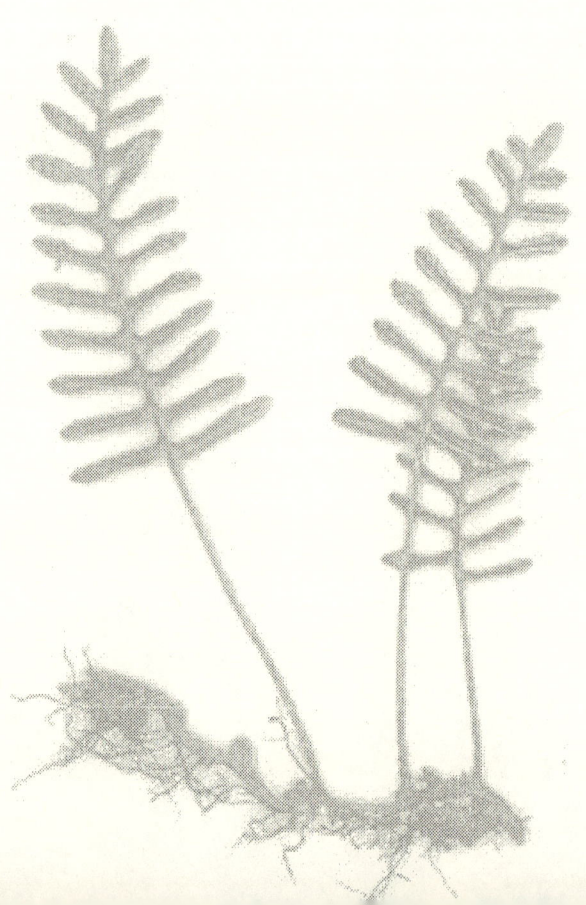

The tendency nowadays to wander in wildernesses is delightful to see. Thousands of tired, nerve-shaken, over-civilized people are beginning to find out that going to the mountains is going home; that wildness is a necessity; and that mountain parks and reservations are useful not only as fountains of timber and irrigating rivers, but as foundations of life.

I stopped one day in San Francisco, and then asked the nearest way out to the untrampled part of the country. "But where do you want to go?" asked the man to whom I had applied for this important information. To any place that is wild," I said.

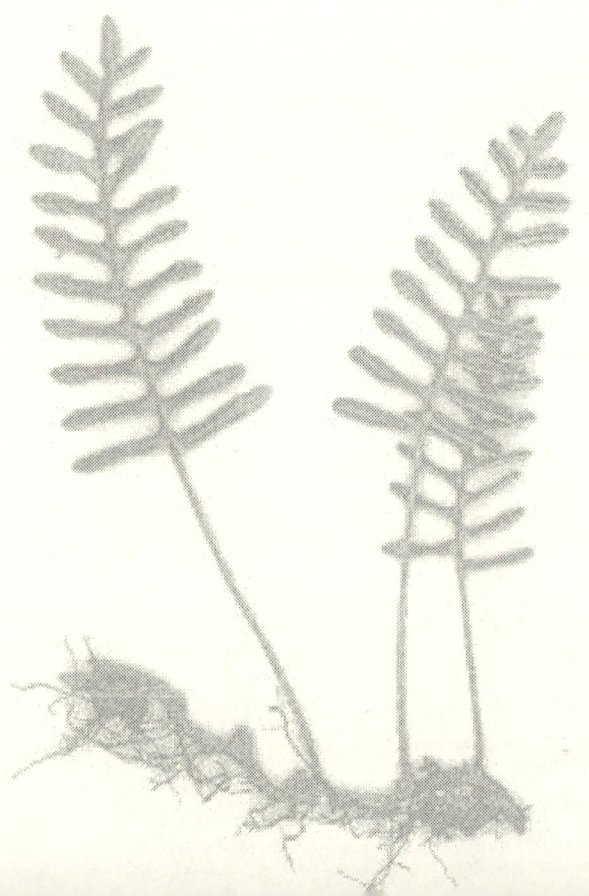

Ho, weary town worker, come to the woods and rest!

As you ascend from the sunny winter of the plain, you find another summer in the foothills of the Sierra; higher up another spring, and on the edge of the valley a snowy winter; descending into the Yosemite Valley, you find another spring, and then glorious summer along the banks of the Merced. Thus, in the space of a week, you pass through all the seasons in this remarkable region.

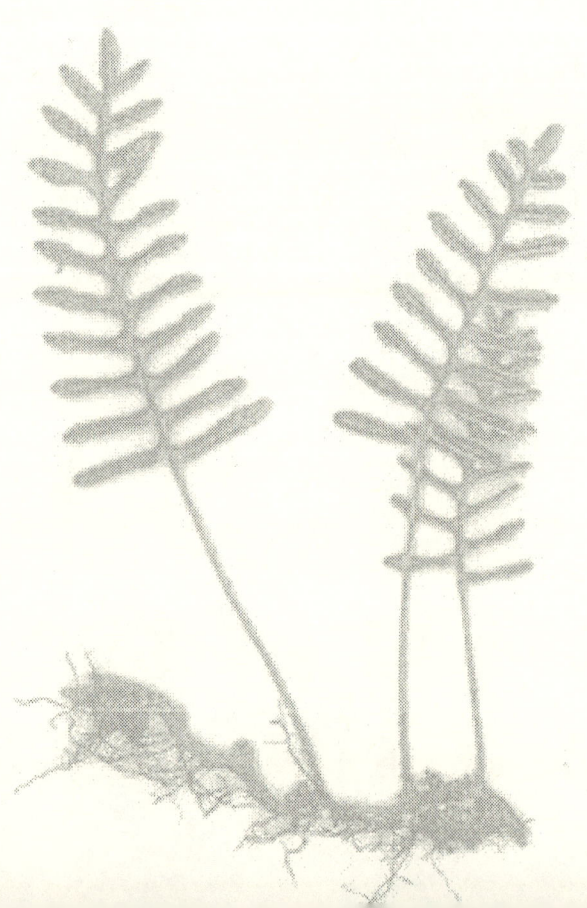

The mountains rise into the cool sky furrowed with canyons almost Yosemite in grandeur, and filled with a glorious profusion of flowers and trees. Lovers of science, lovers of wildness, lovers of pure rest will find here more than they ever may hope for.

Going to the woods is going home; for I suppose we came from the woods originally. But in some of Nature's forests the adventurous traveler seems a feeble, unwelcome creature; wild beasts and the weather trying to kill him, the rank tangled vegetation armed with spears and stinging needles barring his way and making life a hard struggle.

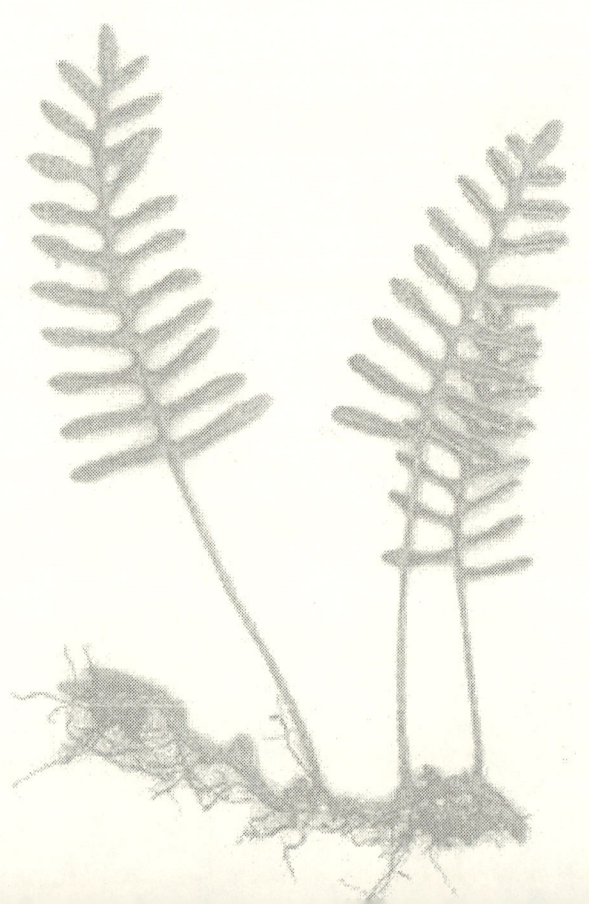

Brooding over some vast mountain landscape, or among the spiritual countenances of mountain flowers, our bodies disappear, our mortal coils come off without any shuffling, and we blend into the rest of Nature, utterly blind to the boundaries that measure human quantities into separate individuals.

> When I reached the valley, all the rocks seemed talkative, and more lovable than ever. They are dear friends, and have warm blood gushing through their granite flesh; and I love them with a love intensified by long and close companionship.

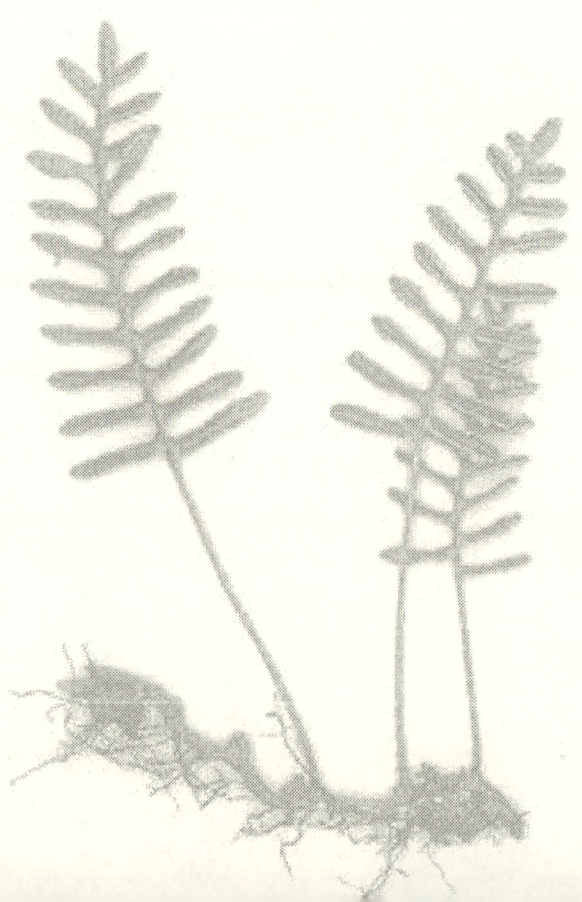

Down through the midst flows the crystal Merced—river of mercy—peacefully gliding, reflecting lilies and trees and the onlooking rocks, things frail and fleeting and types of endurance meeting here and blending in countless forms, as if into this one mountain mansion Nature had gathered her choicest treasures, whether great or small, to draw her lovers into close and confiding communion with her.

In the near foreground is the joyous creek, Tenaya, singing against boulders that are white with the snow. Now, look back twenty yards, and you will see a water-fall, fair as a spirit; the moonlight just touches it, bringing it in relief against the deepest, dark background.

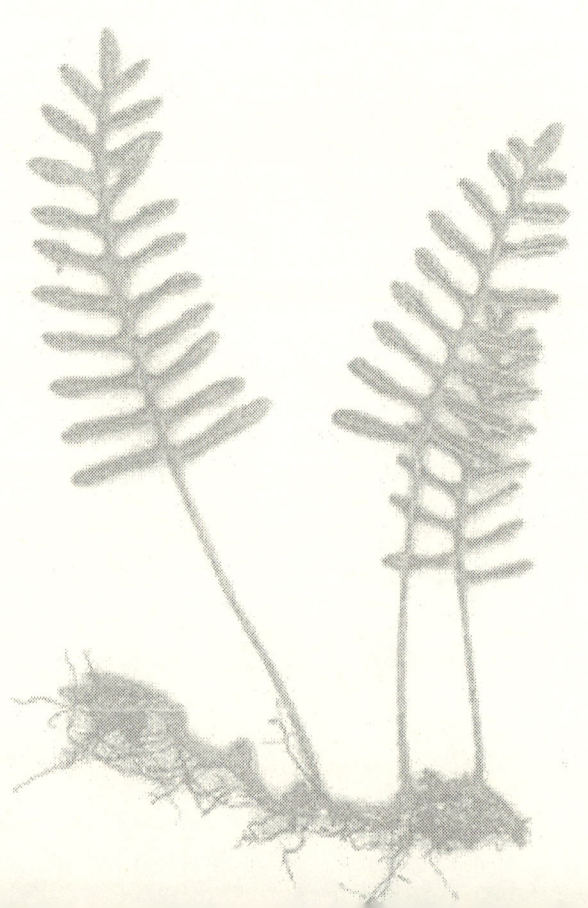

When one comes suddenly out of the woods everything is novel.
The wide arching sky, the flowing plains, fields, dogs, horses, oxen,
are beheld as never seen before, and even our fellow beings
are regarded with something of the same keenness and freshness
of perception that is brought to the study of a new
species of wild animal.

Hummingbirds are among the best and most conspicuous of the mountaineers, flashing their ruby throats in countless wild gardens far up the higher slopes, where they would be least expected. All one has to do to enjoy the company of these mountain-loving midgets is to display a showy blanket or handkerchief.

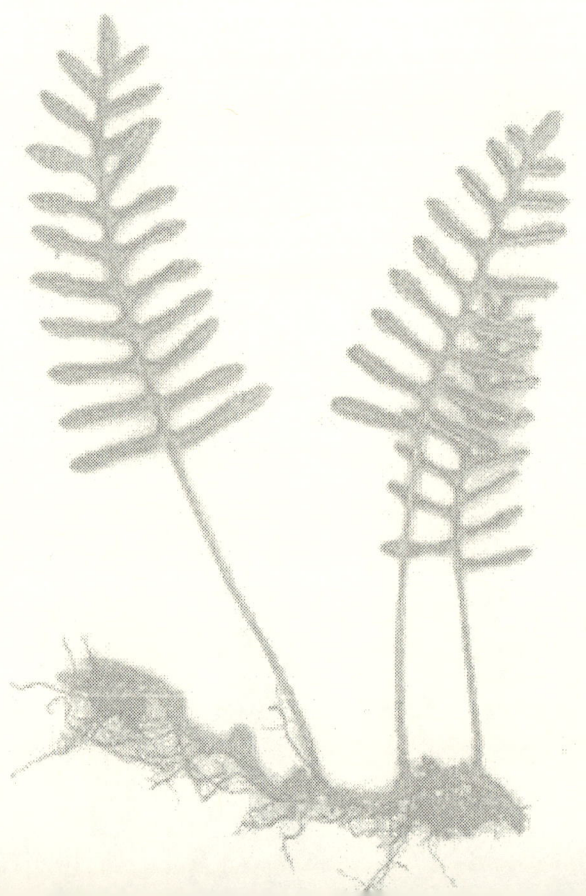

The arctic bluebird is another delightful mountaineer, singing a wild, cherry song and carrying the sky on his back over all the gray ridges and domes of the subalpine region.

Fresh, wild beauty opens one's eyes wherever it is really seen, but the very abundance and completeness of the common beauty that besets our steps, prevents its being absorbed and appreciated. It is a good thing, therefore, to make short excursions now and then to the bottom of the sea among rare dulses of corals, or up beyond the clouds, or even to creep worm-like into dark holes and caverns underground.

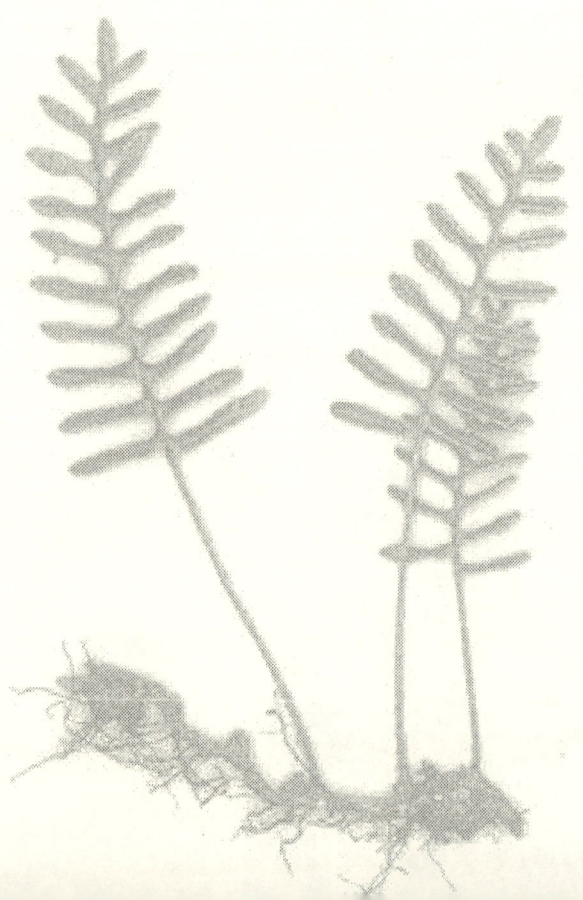

Bears, too, roam the sweet wildness, their blunt, shaggy forms harmonizing well with the trees and tangled bushes, and with the bees, also, notwithstanding the disparity in size. They are fond of all good things, and enjoy them to the utmost, with but little troublesome discrimination—flowers and leaves as well as berries, and the bees themselves as well as their honey.

In my first interview with a Sierra bear we were frightened and embarrassed, both of us, but the bear's behavior was better than mine. When I discovered him, he was standing in a narrow strip of meadow, and I was concealed behind a tree on the side of it. After studying his appearance as he stood at rest, I rushed toward him to frighten him, that I might study his gait in running. But, contrary to all I had heard about the shyness of bears, he did not run at all; and when I stopped short within a few steps of him, as he held his ground in a fighting attitude, my mistake was monstrously plain. I was then put on my good behavior, and never afterward forgot the right manners of the wilderness.

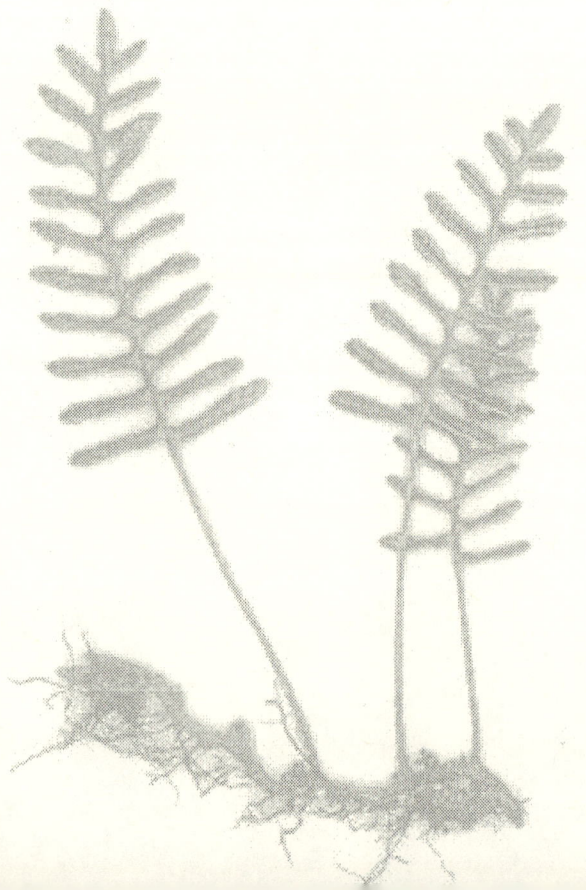

Frogs abound in all the bogs, marshes, pools, and lakes, however cold and high and isolated. How did they manage to get up these high mountains? Surely not by jumping. Long and dry excursions through weary miles of boulders and brush would be trying to frogs. Most likely their stringy spawn is carried on the feet of ducks, cranes, and other waterbirds. Anyhow, they are most thoroughly distributed, and flourish famously. What a cheery, hearty set they are, and how bravely their krink and tronk concerts enliven the rocky wilderness!

I fancied I could see the air whirling in dimpled eddies from sparrow- and lark-wings, earthquake boulders descending in a song of curves, snowflakes glinting songfully hither and thither. "The water in music the oar forsakes." The air in music the wing forsakes. All things move in music and write it. The mouse, lizard, and grasshopper sing together on the Turlock sands, sing with the morning stars.

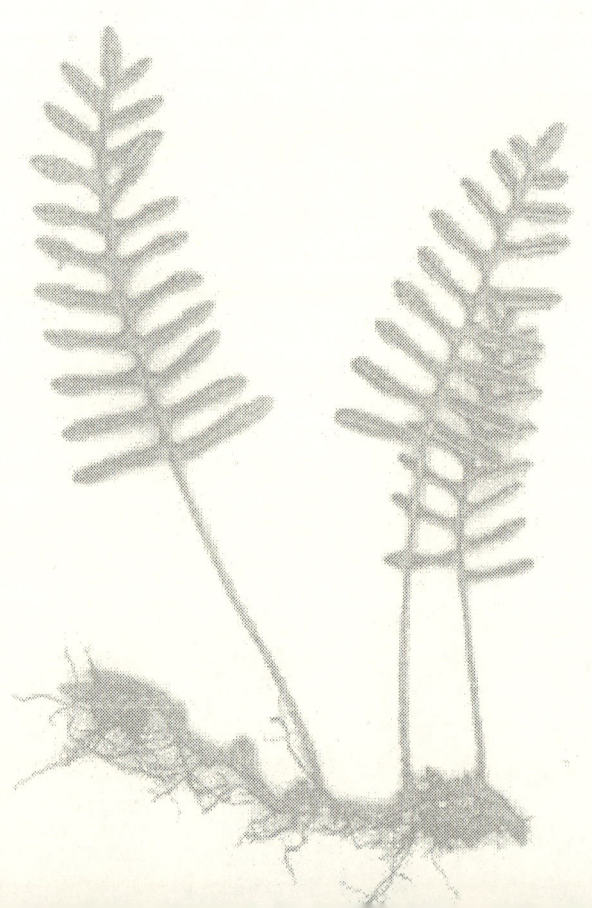

The rocks seem to be completely saturated with color put on and rubbed in with wild audacity without any fear, or caution, or moderation. Mountain masses of paint, millions of tons of it, ever being washed away yet more and more of it coming into sight; the whole effect being so entirely strange and exciting that even a river might be afraid to enter such a place. Nevertheless, here also harmony rules supreme. Linnaea hangs her twin bells over the rugged edges of the cliffs, forests and gardens are spread in lavish beauty roundabout, the nuts and berries ripen well, making good pastures for the birds and bees, and the bears also, and elk, and deer, and buffalo

By forces seemingly antagonistic and destructive, has Mother Nature accomplished her beneficent designs—now a flood of fire, now a flood of ice, now a flood of water; and then an outburst of organic life, a milky-way of snowy petals and wings, girdling the rugged mountain like a cloud, as if the vivifying sunbeams beating against its sides had broken into a foam of plant-bloom and bees.

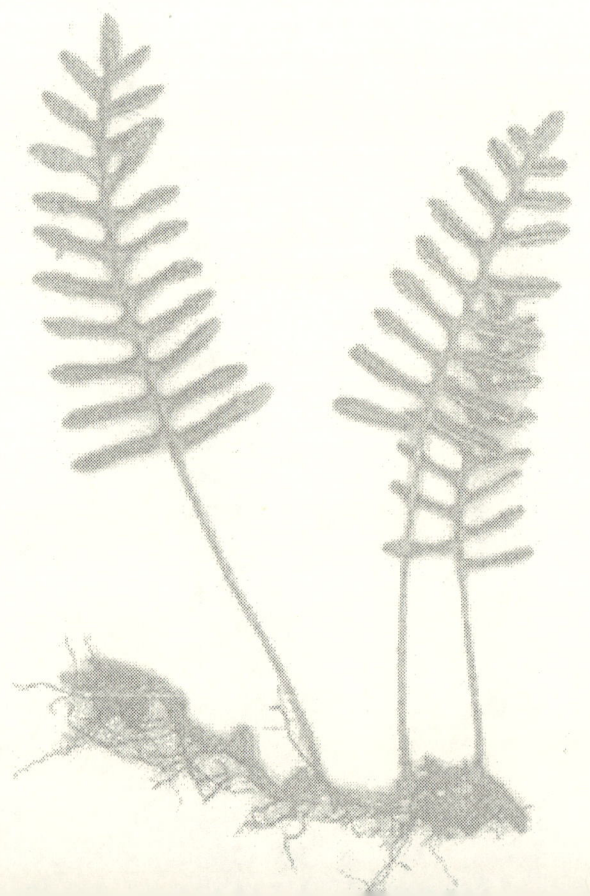

Near the Roaring Fall we came to a little circular meadow which was one of the most perfect gardens I ever saw. It was planted with lilies and orchids, larkspurs and columbines, daisies and asters, and sun-loving goldenrods, violets, brier-roses, and purple geranium, and a hundred others whose names no one would care to read, though everybody would surely love them at first sight.

Day after day we seem to float in the very heart of true fairyland, each succeeding view seeming more and more beautiful, the one we chance to have before us the most surprisingly beautiful of all.

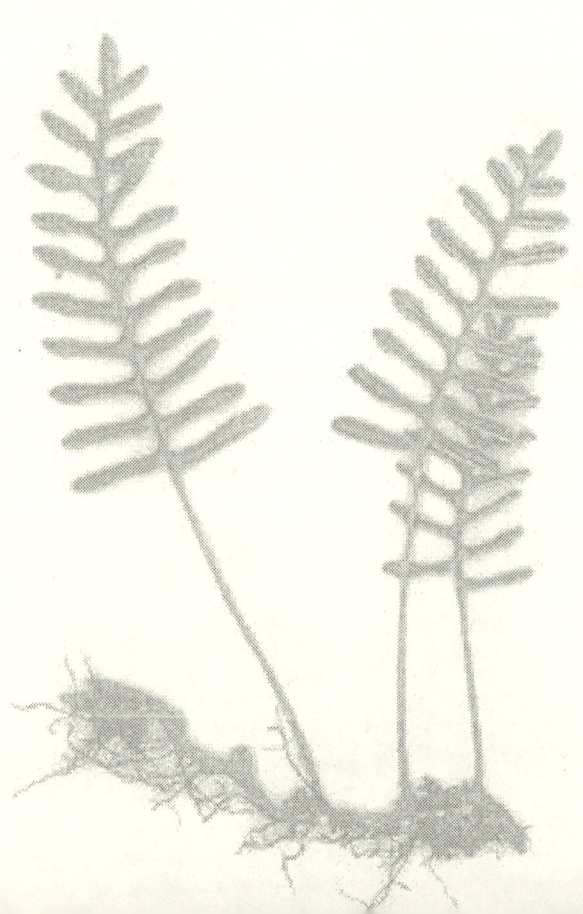

The lake is fairly blooming in purple light, and is so responsive to the sky, both in calmness and color, that it seems itself a sky.

The alpenglow is fading into earthy, murky gloom, but do not let your town habits draw you away to the hotel. Stay on this good fire-mountain and spend the night among the stars. Watch their glorious bloom until the dawn, and get one more baptism of light. Then, with fresh heart, go down to your work, and whatever your fate, under whatever ignorance or knowledge you may afterward chance to suffer, you will remember these fine, wild views, and look back with joy to your wanderings.

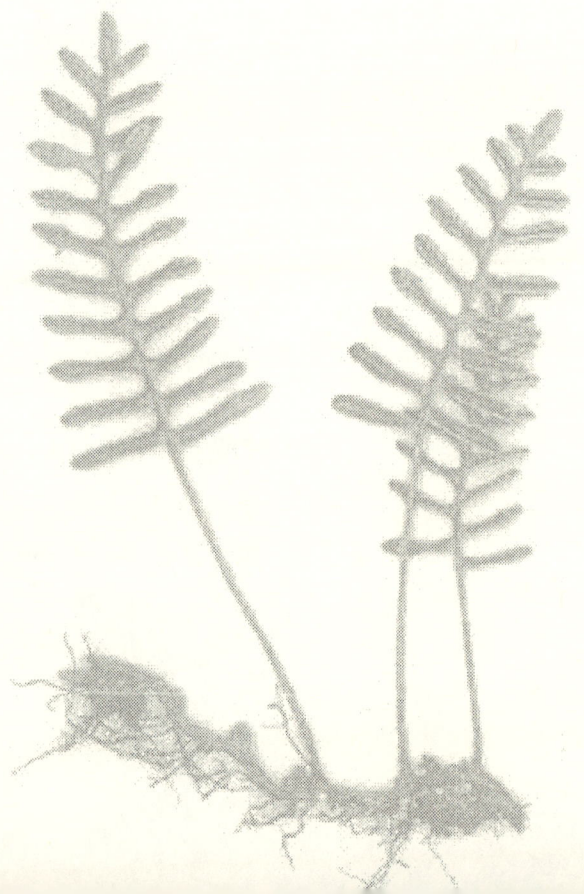

The water-ground chips and knots that I found fastened between rocks, kept my fire alive all through the night, and I rose nerved and ready for another day of sketching and noting, and any form of climbing.

When, like a merchant taking a list of his goods, we take stock of our wildness, we are glad to see how much of even the most destructible kind is still unspoiled. Looking at our continent as scenery when it was all wild, lying between beautiful seas, the starry sky above it, the starry rocks beneath it, to compare its sides, the East and the West, would be like comparing the sides of a rainbow.

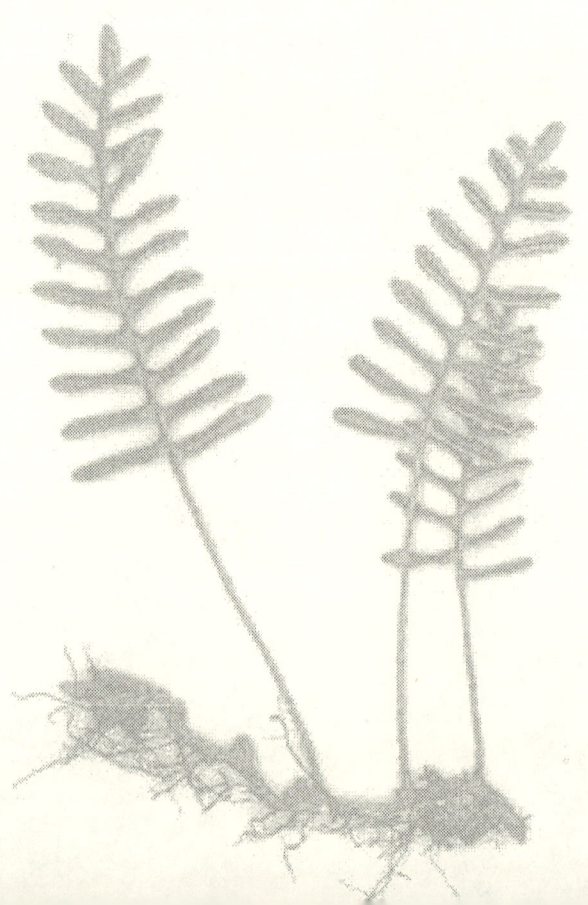

If people in general could be got into the woods, even for once, to hear the trees speak for themselves, all difficulties in the way of forest preservation would vanish.

When a man plants a tree he plants himself. Every root is an anchor, over which he rests with grateful interest, and becomes sufficiently calm to feel the joy of living. He necessarily makes the acquaintance of the sun of the sky. Favorite trees fill his mind, and while tending them like children, and accepting the benefits they bring, becomes himself a benefactor.

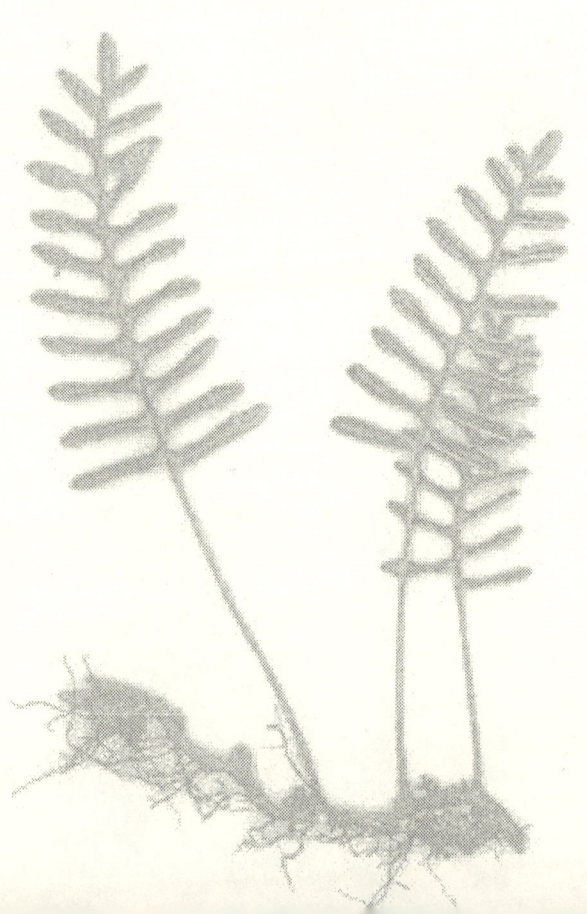

Rest pays even in a pecuniary way, for one will do more and better work in a lifetime by taking a good summer Sabbath every year; and those Sabbath months, in the total length of one's life, will rather be added, with good compound interest at the end.

In going across to the river, I had a suggestive time, breaking my way through tangles of blackberry and brier-rose, and willow. I admire delicate plants that are well prickled, and, therefore, took my scratched face and hands patiently. I bathed in the sacred stream, seeming to catch all its mountain tones while it softly murmured and rippled over the shallows of brown pebbles. The whole river, back to its icy sources, seemed to rise in clear vision with its countless cascades, and falls, and blooming meadows, and gardens.

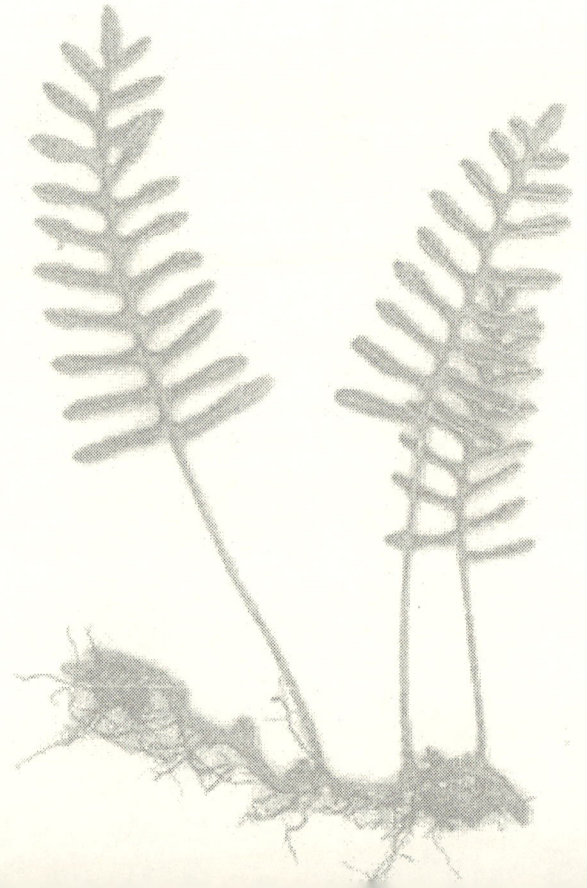

One of the tiger lilies that I measured was six feet long, and had eleven open flowers, five of them in prime beauty. The wind rocked this splendid orange panicle above the heads of the geraniums and briar roses, forming a spectacle of pure beauty exquisitely poised and harmonized in all its parts. It was as if Nature had fingered every leaf and petal that very day, readjusting every curve, and touching the colors of every corolla; and so she had, for not a leaf was misbent, and every plant was so placed with reference to every other in form and color that the whole garden had evidently been arranged like one tasteful bouquet. Here I lived a fine unmeasured hour "considering the lilies," warming among the mellow waving golden rods, and gazing into the countenances of the briars and small white violets.

Farther on, a harsh grunting and growling seemed to come from the opposite bank of a brook along which we rode. "What? Hush! That's a bear," ejaculated Black, in a gruff, bearish undertone. "Yes," he said, "some rough old Bruin is sauntering this fine night, seeking some wayside sheep lost from migrating flocks." Of course, all night-sounds, otherwise unaccountable, are accredited to bears. On ascending a sloping hillock, less than a mile from the first, we heard another grunting bear, but whether or not daylight would transform our bears to pigs, may well be counted into the story.

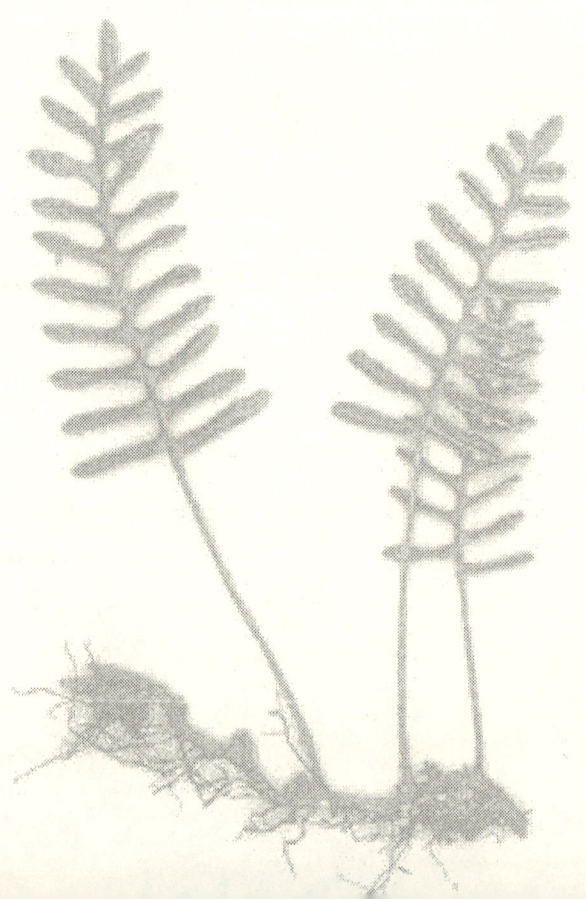

The summer day died in purple and gold, and we lay watching the growing shadows and the fading sunglow among the heights. Each member of the party made his own bed, like birds building nests. Mine was made of fern fronds, with a sprinkling of mint spikes in the pillow, thus combining luxurious softness with delicate fragrance, in which one sleeps not only restfully but deliciously, making the down beds of palaces and palace hotels seem poor and vulgar by contrast.

The full moon rose just after the night darkness was fairly established. The dim gray cliff at the foot of which we lay was crowned with an arch of white, cold light long before the moon's disc appeared above the opposite wall. Down the valley one rock-front after another caught the silvery glow, and came out from [the] gray and dusky shadows in long, imposing ranks, like very spirits, forming altogether one of the most impressive scenes I ever beheld. The tranquil sky was also intensely lovely, blooming with stars like a meadow, and the thickets and groves along the river bank were masses of solid darkness.

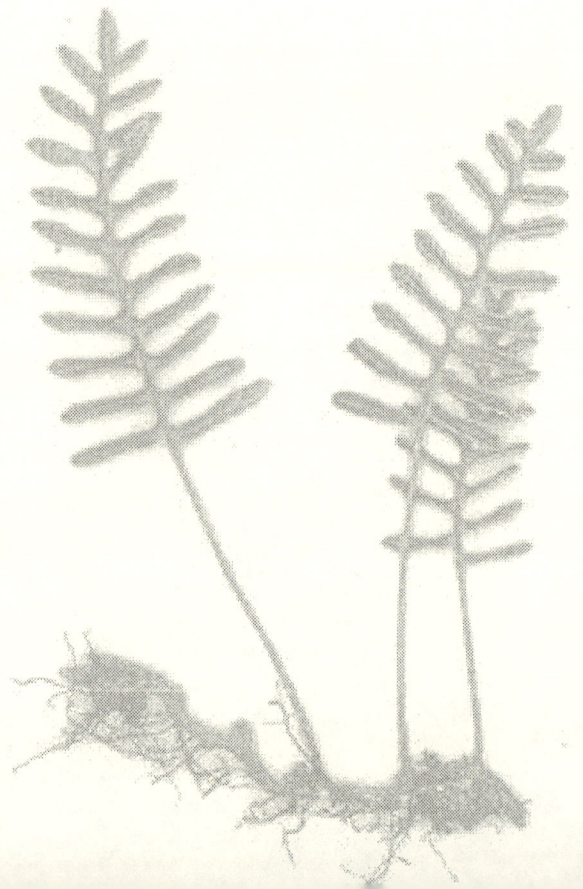

The influences of pure Nature are as yet so little known, that it is generally supposed that complete pleasure of this kind, permeating one's very flesh and bones, unfits the student for scientific pursuits in which cool judgment and observation are required. But the effect is just the opposite of this. Instead of producing a dissipated condition, the mind is fertilized and stimulated and developed like sun-fed plants.

One morning when I was eating breakfast in a little garden spot on the Kaweah, hedged around with chaparral, I noticed a deer's head thrust through the bushes, the big beautiful eyes gazing at me. I kept still, and the deer ventured forward a step, then snorted and withdrew. In a few minutes she returned, and came into the open garden, stepping with infinite grace, followed by two others. After showing themselves for a moment, they bounded over the hedge with sharp, timid snorts and vanished. But curiosity brought them back with still another, and all four came into my garden, and, satisfied that I meant them no ill, began to feed, actually eating breakfast with me.

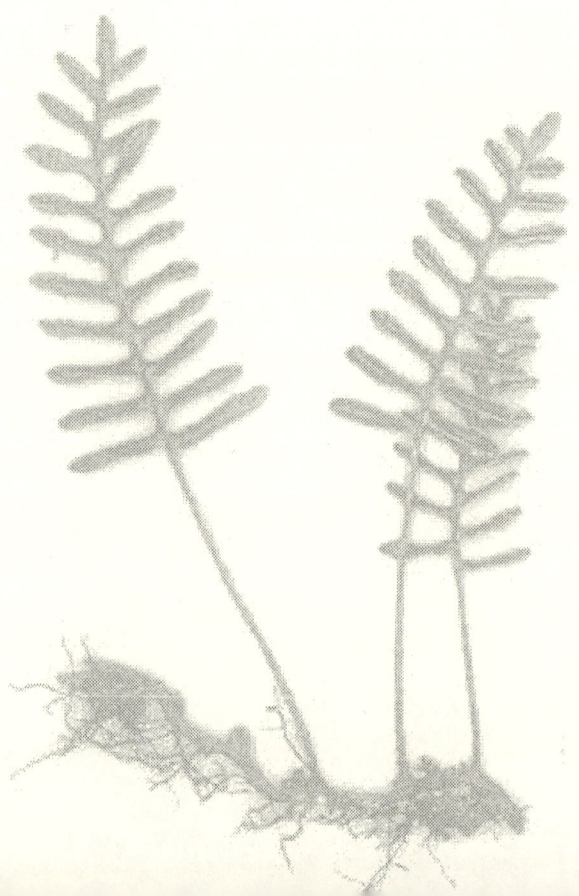

In one spot I found an opening in the thorny sky where I could stand erect, and on the further side of the opening discovered a small pool. "Now here," I said, "I must be careful in creeping for the birds of the neighborhood come here to drink, and the rattlesnakes come here to catch them." I then began to cast my eye along the channel, instinctively feeling a snakey atmosphere, and finally discovered one rattler between my feet. But there was a bashful look in his eye, and a withdrawing, deprecating kink in his neck that showed plainly as words could tell that he would not strike, and only wished to be let alone.

In every walk with Nature one receives far more than they seek.

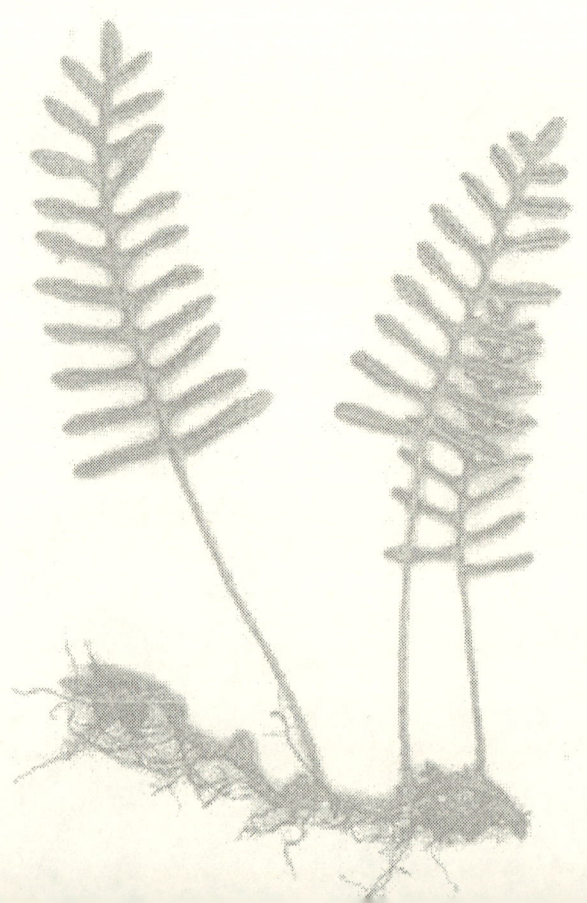

Benevolent, solemn, fateful, pervaded with divine light, every landscape glows like a countenance hallowed in eternal repose; and every one of its living creatures, clad in flesh and leaves, and every crystal of its rocks, whether on the surface shining in the sun or buried miles deep in what we call darkness, is throbbing and pulsing with the heartbeats of God.

To everybody over all the world water is beautiful forever, whether falling upward into the sky in snowy geysers, or downward into deep resounding canyons, or gliding and resting in calm rivers and lakes. Through frost or fire, tranquil or in storm, massed in seas or in drops of dew, or drifting in clouds on the mountains; through all its forms forever and forever water is beautiful.

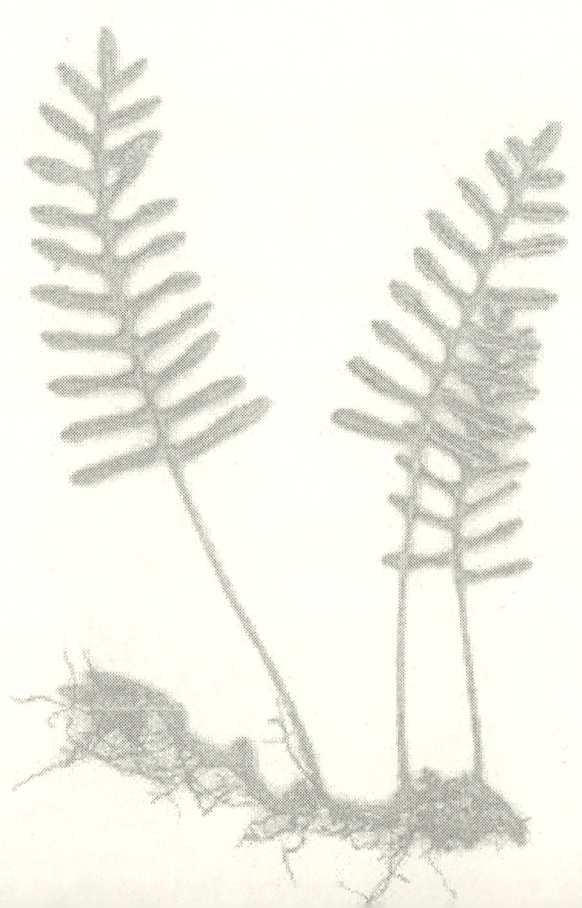

Anxious to learn what I could about the structure of this curious ice-hill, I tried to climb it, carrying an ax to cut footsteps. Before I had reached the base of it I was met by a current of spray and wind that made breathing difficult. I pushed on backward, however, and soon gained the slope of the hill, where by creeping close to the surface most of the blast was avoided. Thus I made my way nearly to the summit, halting at times to peer up through the wild whirls of spray, or to listen to the sublime thunder beneath me, the whole hill sounding as if it were a huge, bellowing, exploding drum. I hoped that by waiting until the fall was blown aslant I should be able to climb to the lip of the crater and get a view of the interior; but a suffocating blast, half air, half water, followed by the fall of an enormous mass of ice from the wall, quickly discouraged me. The whole cone was jarred by the blow, and I was afraid its side might fall in. Some fragments of the mass sped past me dangerously near; so I beat a hasty retreat, chilled and drenched, and laid myself on a sunny rock in a safe place to dry.

I was soon separated from my companion and left alone, and as the twilight began to fall I sat down on the mossy instep of a spruce. Not a bush or tree was moving, every leaf seemed hushed in deep brooding repose. One bird, a thrush, sang, silently lancing the silence with his cheery notes and making it all the more keenly felt, while the solemn monotone of the stream sifted through all the air, pervading every pore like the very voice of God, humanized, terrestrialized, and coming into one's heart as to a home prepared for it.

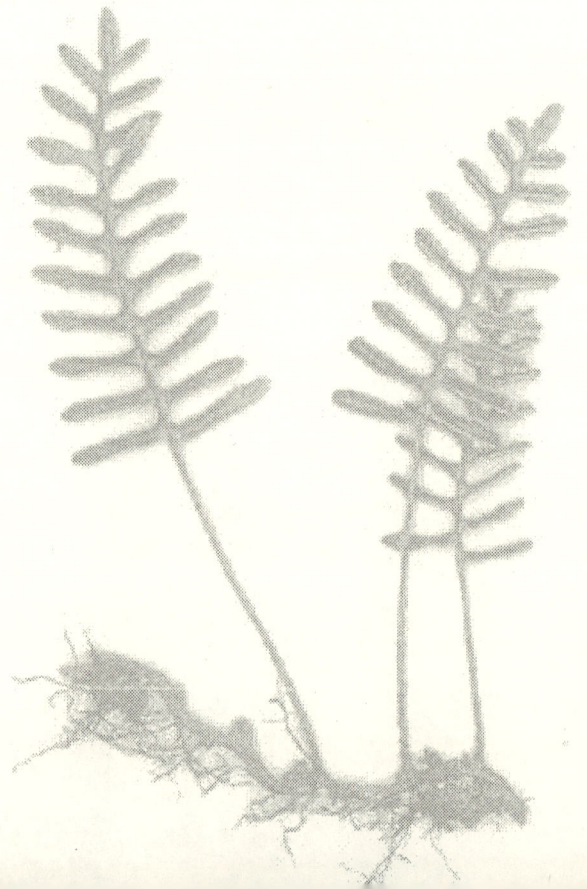

As the night advanced, the mighty rocks of my mountain mansion seemed to come nearer. The starry sky stretched across from wall to wall like a ceiling, and fitted closely down into all the spiky irregularities of the summits.

> My own ways are easily made, for my mountaineering has heretofore been almost wholly accomplished on foot, carrying a minimum of every necessity, and lying down by any streamside whenever overtaken by weariness and night.

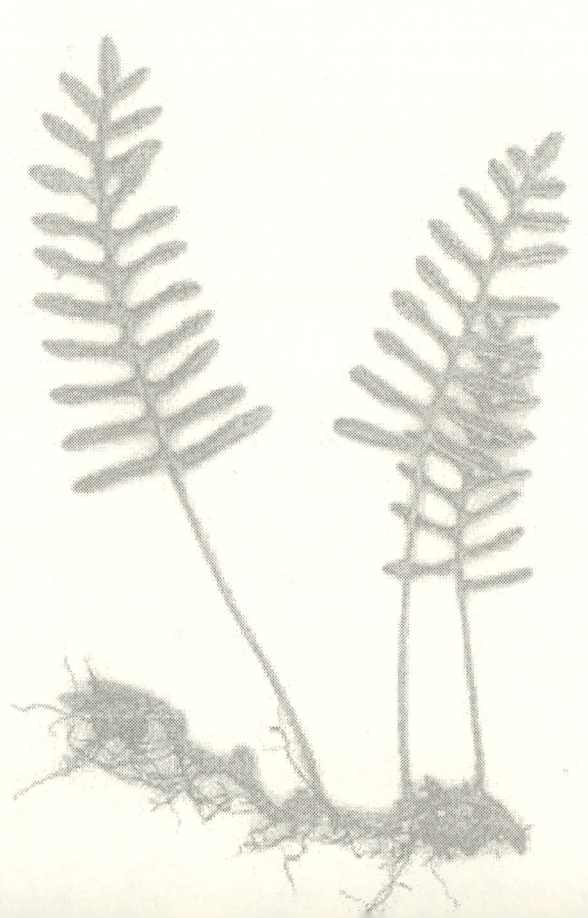

The creative sun shone gloriously upon the white expanse, and rare cloud-lands, hill and dale, mountain and valley, rose responsive to his rays, and steadily developed to higher beauty and individuality.

One morning I was awakened by the pelting of pine cones on the roof of my cabin, and found, on going out, that the north wind had taken possession of the valley, filling it with a sea-like roar, and arousing the pines to magnificent action, made them bow like supple willows. The valley had been visited a short time before by a succession of most beautiful snowstorms, and the floor, and the cliffs, and all the region round about were lavishly laden with winter jewelry. Rocks, trees, the sandy flats and the meadows, all were in bloom, and the air was filled with a dust of shining petals. The gale increased all day, and branches and tassels and empty burs of the silver pine covered the snow, while the falls were being twisted and torn and tossed about as if they were mere wisps of floating mist.

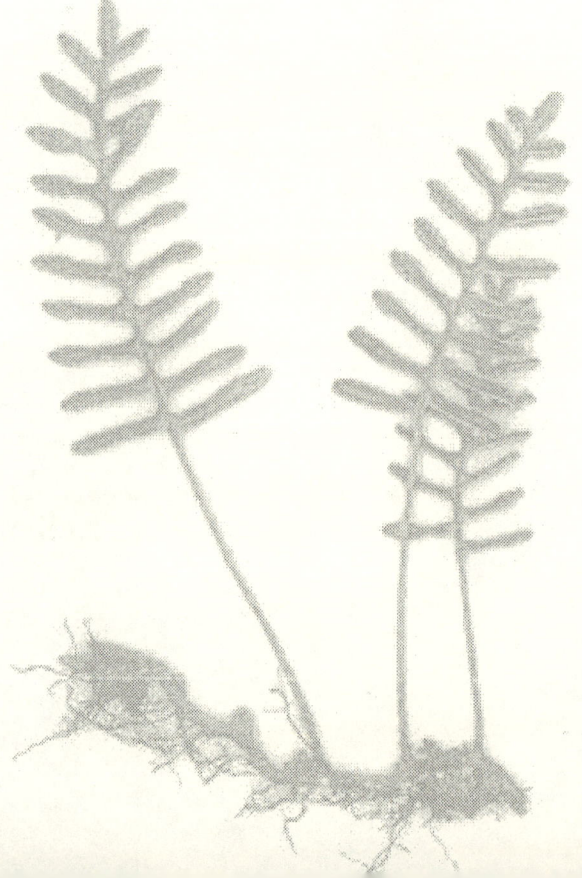

Nature is seldom suspected of being poor, for does she not possess all the real estate of the world, to say nothing of unexplored moons and stars?

The voice of the fall was now low, and the grand flood had waned to floating gauze and thin-broidered folds of linked and arrowy lace-work. When I reached the fall slant sunbeams were glinting across the head of it, leaving all the rest in shadow; and on the illumined brow a group of yellow spangles were playing, of singular form and beauty, flashing up and dancing in large flame-shaped masses, wavering at times, then steadying, rising and falling in accord with the shifting forms of the water. But the color changed not at all. Nothing in clouds or flowers, on bird-wings or the lips of shells, could rival it in fineness. It was the most divinely beautiful mass of yellow light I ever beheld—one of Nature's precious sights that come to us but once in a lifetime.

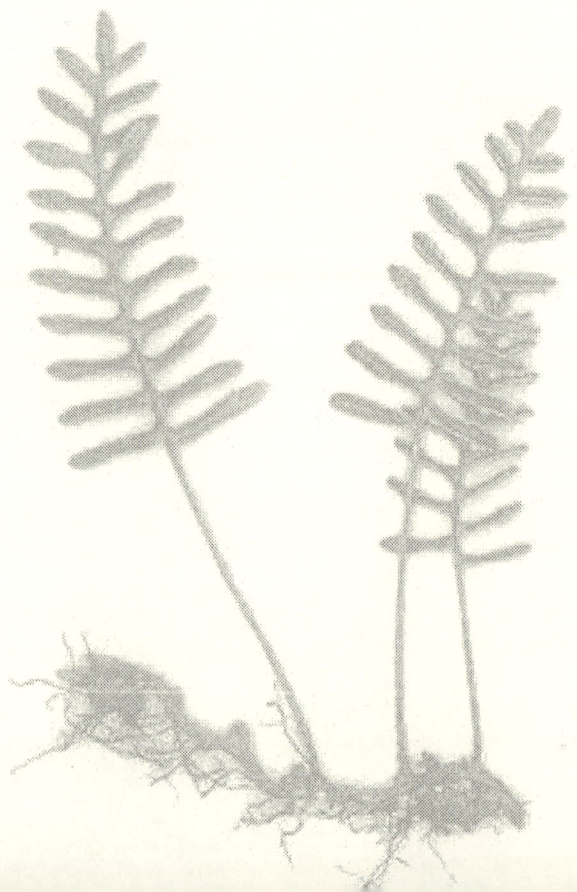

Down came a dash of spent comets, thin and harmless-looking
in the distance, but desperately solid and stony when they struck
my shoulders, like a mixture of choking spray and gravel and big
hailstones. Instinctively dropping on my knees, I gripped an angle
of the rock, curled up like a young fern frond, with my face pressed
against my breast, and in this attitude submitted
as best I could to my thundering bath.

> Thousands of God's wild blessings will search you and soak you as if you were a sponge, and the big days will go by uncounted.

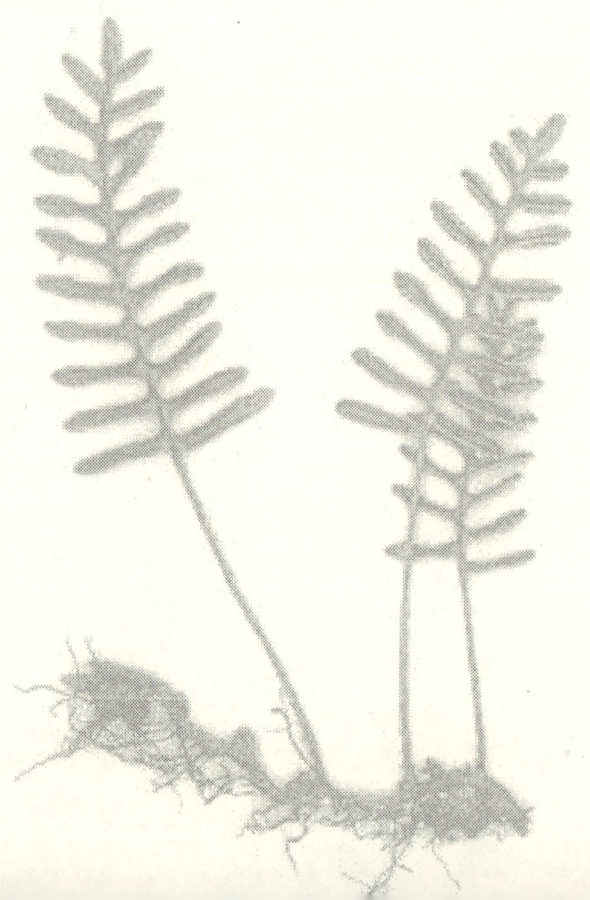

The toning spiciness and richness of these forests after rain can never be described. The flowers, and buds, and leaves of every thing that grows are steeped and made into tea. Pines, with their sugar, and gum and rosins; firs, with spicy balsam; pungent spruces and junipers; mossy bogs and flowery meadows, all soaked together as if in one pot, fairly filling the sky with a subtle, invigorating aroma.

The rain brought out all the colors of the woods with the most delightful freshness—the rich browns of bark, and burs, and fallen leaves, and dead forms; the grays of rocks and lichens; the light purple of swelling buds, and the fine warm yellow greens of mosses and libocedrus. The air was steaming with fragrance, not rising and wafting past in separate masses, but equally diffused throughout all the wind.

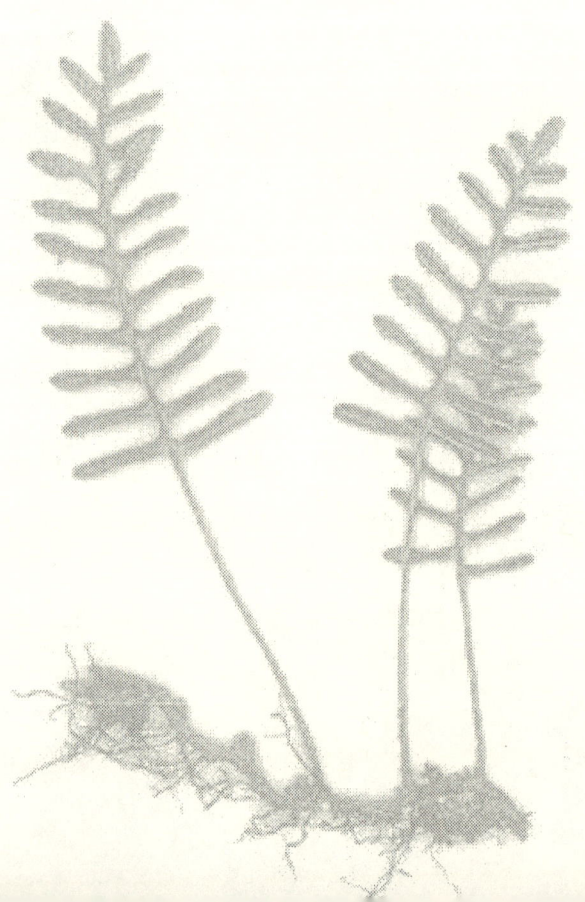

How interesting would be the history of a single rain-drop followed back from the ground to its farthest fountains.

How glorious a greeting the sun gives the mountains! To behold this alone is worth the pains of any excursion a thousand times over. The highest peaks burned like islands in a sea of liquid shade. Then the lower peaks and spires caught the glow, and long lances of light, streaming through many a notch and pass, fell thick on the frozen meadows.

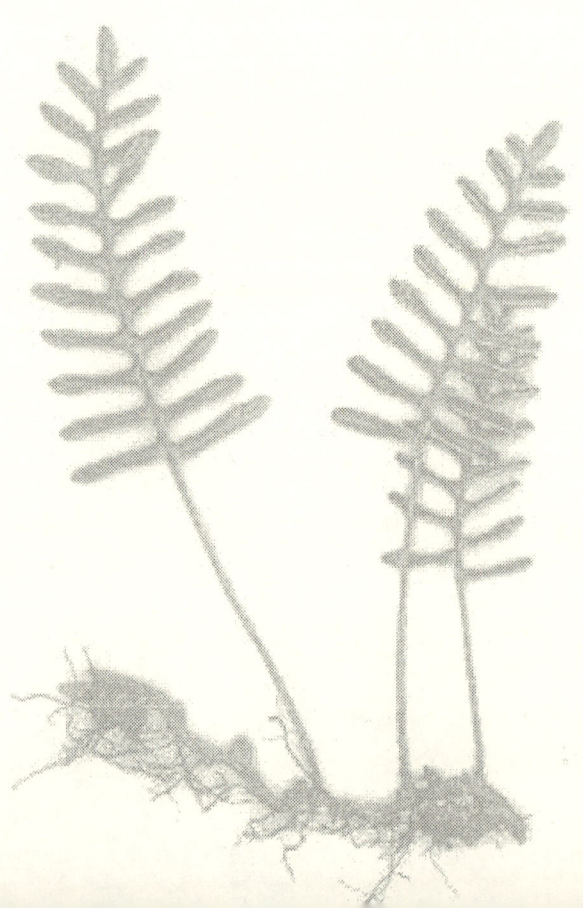

Briskly venturing and roaming, some are washing off sins and cobweb cares of the devil's spinning in all-day storms on mountains; sauntering in rosiny pinewoods or in gentian meadows, brushing through chaparral, bending down and parting sweet, flowery sprays; tracing rivers to their sources, getting in touch with the nerves of Mother Earth; jumping from rock to rock, feeling the life of them, learning the songs of them, panting in whole-souled exercise and rejoicing in deep, long-drawn breaths of pure wildness.

In every country the mountains are fountains, not only of rivers but of men. Therefore we all are born mountaineers, the offspring of rock and sunshine; and, although according to ordinary commercial methods of computation it may seem a long way down through lichen and pinetree to God-like human beings, yet measured by other standards the distance becomes scarcely appreciable.

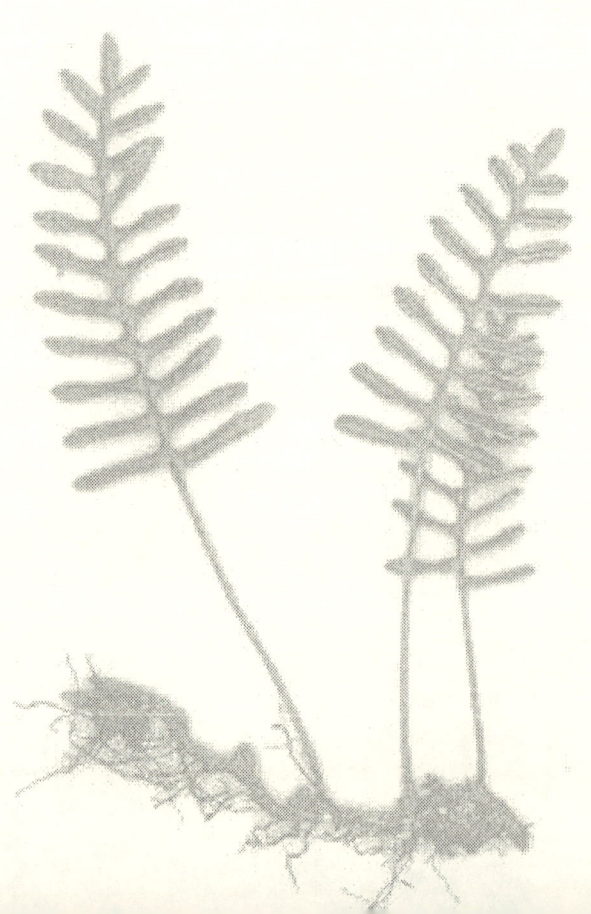

Storm clouds on the mountains—how truly beautiful they are!—
floating fountains bearing water for every well; the angels
of streams and lakes; brooding in the deep pure azure,
or sweeping along the ground, over ridge and dome, over
meadow, over forest, over garden and grove; lingering with
cooling shadows, refreshing every flower, and soothing rugged
rock brows with a gentleness of touch and gesture
no human hand can equal!

> Going to the mountains is going home, and gladly we climbed higher, higher, through the freshened piney woods—over meadows, over streamlets, over waving ridge and dome.

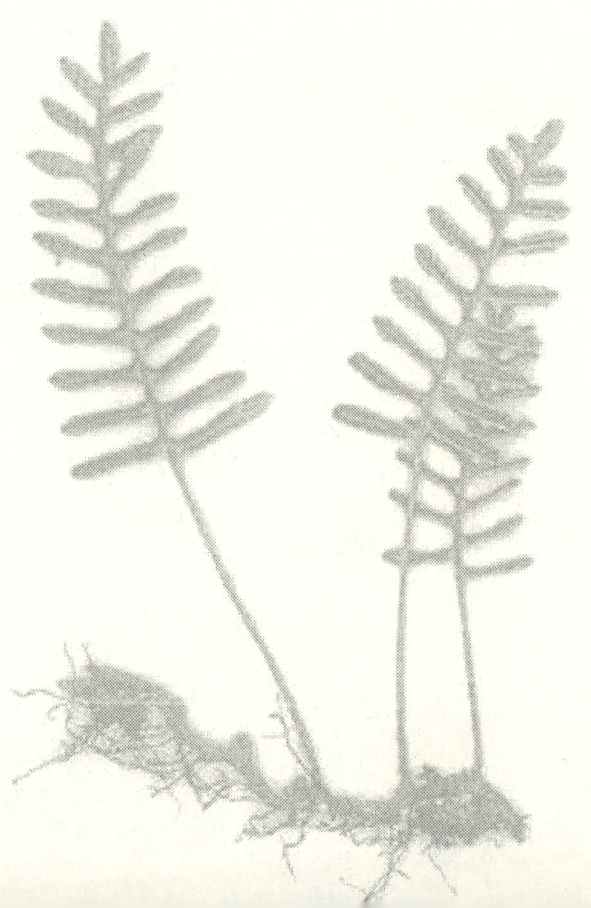

All Nature's wildness tells the same story: the shocks and outbursts of earthquakes, volcanoes, geysers, roaring, thundering waves and floods, the silent uprush of sap in plants, storms of every sort, each and all, are the orderly, beauty-making love-beats of Nature's heart.

The practical importance of the preservation of our forests is augmented by their relations to climate, soil and streams. Strip off the woods, with their underbrush from the mountain flanks, and the whole State, the lowlands as well as the highlands, would gradually change into a desert.

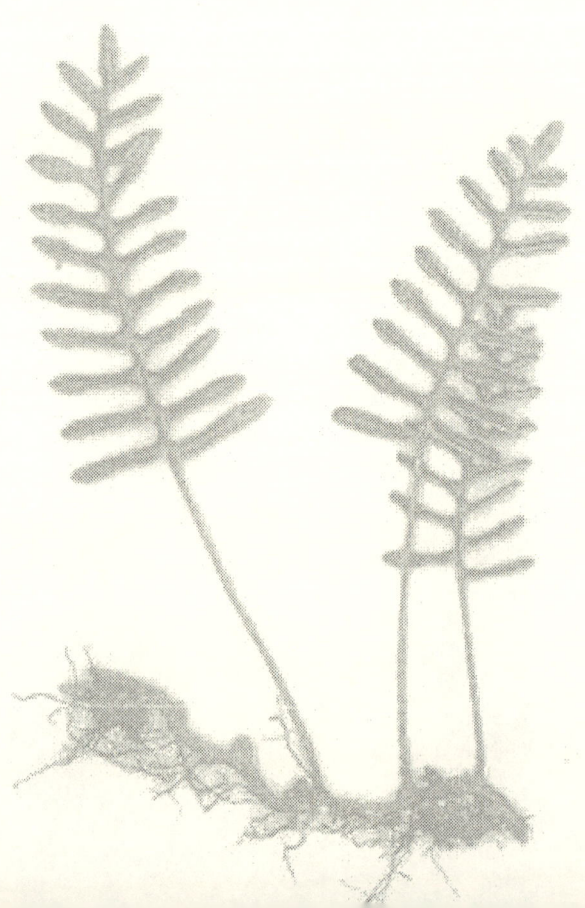

Earth and sky, round and round the entire landscape, was one ravishing revelation of color, infinitely varied and interblended. I have seen many a glorious sunset beneath lifting storm clouds on the mountains, but nothing comparable with this.

I chose a camping ground for the night down on the brink of a glacier lake, where a thicket of Williamson spruce sheltered me from the night wind. After making a tin-cupful of tea, I sat by my camp fire, reflecting on the grandeur and significance of the glacial record I had seen, and speculating on the developments of the morrow.

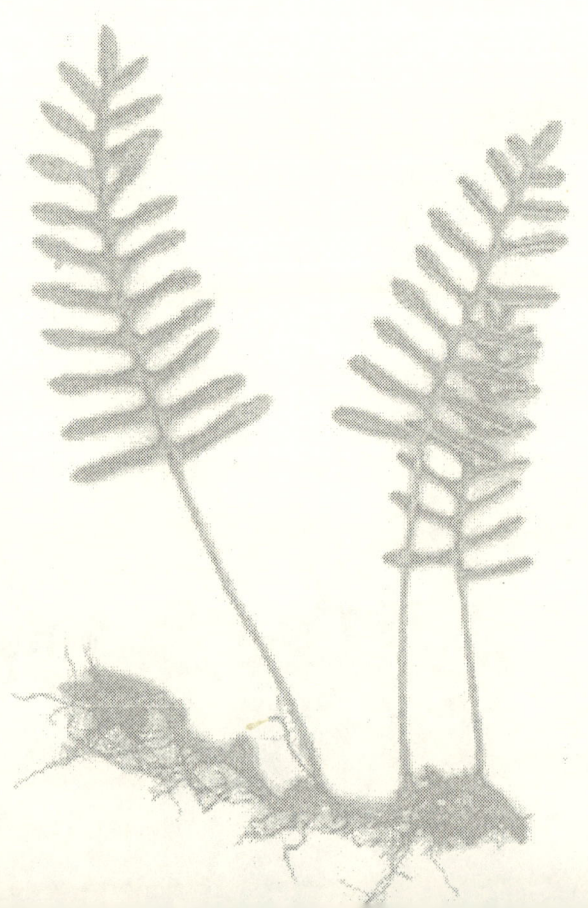

How wholly infused with God is this one big word of love that we call the world! Goodnight. Do you see the fire-glow on my icy-smoothed slab, and on my two ferns? And do you hear how sweet a sleep-song the fall and cascade are singing?

After a long fireside rest and a glance at my field-notes, I cut a few pine tassels for a bed, and fell into the clear death-like sleep that always comes to the tired mountaineer.

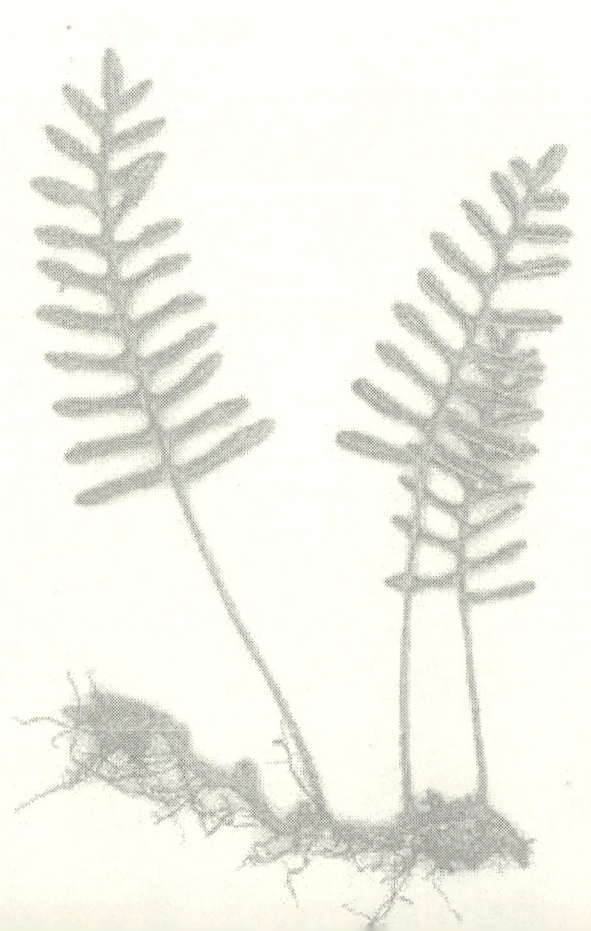

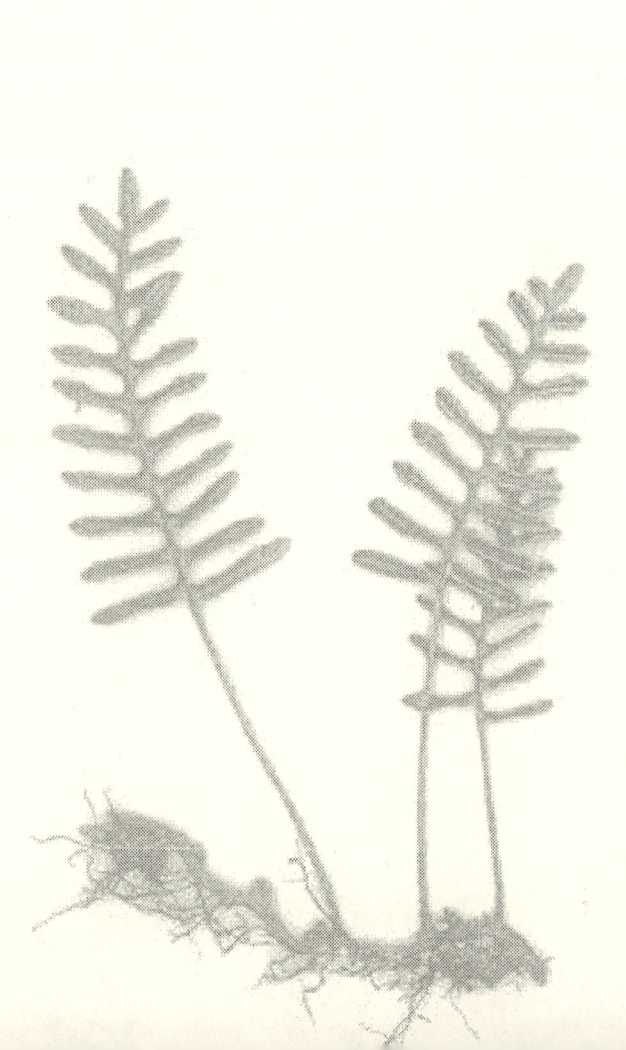

JOHN MUIR'S QUOTES WERE TAKEN FROM THE FOLLOWING ARTICLES.

AM – *The Atlantic Monthly*
BR – *Boston Recorder*
CR – *The Craftsman*
CM – *The Century Magazine*
HNMM – *Harper's New Monthly Magazine*
LWBL – *Library of the World's Best Literature*
NYDT – *New York Daily Tribune*
ON – *Old and New*
OM – *The Overland Monthly*
PBSNH – *Proceedings of the Boston Society of Natural History*
SCB – *Sierra Club Bulletin*
SDU – *Sacramento Daily Union*
SFDEB – *San Francisco Daily Evening Bulletin*
SFDEBS – *San Francisco Daily Evening Bulletin Supplement*
SFE – *The San Francisco Examiner*
SM – *Scribner's Monthly*
WHC – *Woman's Home Companion*

"The Passes of the Sierra," SM, March, 1879.
"John Muir: Geologist, Explorer, Naturalist," CR, March, 1905.
"Flood-Storm in the Sierra," OM, June, 1875.
"Rambles of a Botanist Among the Plants and Climates of California," ON, June, 1872.
"A Wind Storm in the Forests of the Yuba," SM, November, 1878.
"The National Parks and Forest Reservations," SCB, January, 1896.
"Summering in the Sierra," SFDEB, August 3, 1875.
"Summering in the Sierra," SFDEB, August 3, 1875.
"Wild Wool," OM, April, 1875.
"The Yellowstone Park," SFDEB, October 27, 1885.
"Wild Wool," OM, April, 1875.
"The Glacier Meadows of the Sierra," SM, February, 1879.
"Yosemite Valley in Flood," OM, April, 1872.
"The Passes of the Sierra," SM, March, 1879.
"Snow Banners of the California Alps," HNMM, July, 1877.
"In the Heart of the California Alps," SM, July, 1880.
"Cathedral Peak and the Tuolumne Meadows," SCB, January, 1911.
"In the Heart of the California Alps," SM, July, 1880.
"Exploration in the Great Tuolumne Cañon," OM, August, 1873.
"Wild Wool," OM, April, 1875.
"Yosemite National Park," AM, August, 1899.
"Shasta Bees. A Honeyful Region," SFDEB, January 5, 1875.
"The Hetch-Hetchy Valley," SCB, January, 1908.

"A New Top Notch for the Sons of Daniel Boone," WHC, October, 1907.
"For the Boston Recorder. The CALYPSO BOREALIS," BR, December 21, 1866.
"Linnaeus," LWBL, 1896.
"The Treasure of the Yosemite," CM, August, 1890.
"The Glacier Meadows of the Sierra," SM, February, 1879.
"Shasta Bees. A Honeyful Region," SFDEB, January 5, 1875.
"A Geologist's Winter Walk," OM, April, 1873.
"A Letter from the Yosemite Valley," CR, March, 1905.
"In the Heart of the California Alps," SM, July, 1880.
"In the Heart of the California Alps," SM, July, 1880.
"Exploration in the Great Tuolumne Cañon," OM, August, 1873.
"Mount Whitney. Its Ascent by John Muir, the Explorer and Geologist," SFDEB, August, 24, 1875.
"The Corwin's Cruise," SFDEB, June 20, 1881.
"A Rival of the Yosemite," CM, November, 1891.
"Summering in the Sierra," SFDEB, August, 1875.
"Snow Storm on Mount Shasta," HNMM, September, 1877.
"The American Forests," AM, August, 1897.
"The American Forests," AM, August, 1897.
"John Muir: Geologist, Explorer, Naturalist," CR, March, 1905.
"A Sierra Flood Storm," SFDEBS, May 22, 1875.
"Summering in the Sierra," SFDEB, June 24, 1875.
"Summering in the Sierra," SFDEB, August 12, 1876.
"Yosemite in Spring," NYDT, July 11, 1872.
"Among the Birds of Yosemite," AM, December, 1898.
"A Letter from the Yosemite Valley," CR, March, 1905.
"The Grand Cañon of the Colorado," CM, November, 1902.
"The Passes of the Sierra," SM, March, 1879.
"Alaska Glaciers," SFDEB, September 27, 1879.
"Yellowstone National Park," AM, April, 1898.
"Snow Storm on Mount Shasta," HNMM, September, 1877.
"A Geologist's Winter Walk," OM, April, 1873.
"In the Heart of the California Alps," SM, July, 1880.
"A Geologist's Winter Walk," OM, April, 1873.
"In the Heart of the California Alps," SM, July, 1880.
"Yosemite National Park," AM, August, 1899.
"Wild Wool," OM, April, 1875.
"Wild Wool," OM, April, 1875.
"Trails of the Gold Hunters," SFE, October 1, 1897.
"Wild Sheep of the Sierra," SM, May, 1881.
"Mormon Lilies," SFDEB, July 19, 1877.
"Trails of the Gold Hunters," SFE, October 1, 1897.
"Trails of the Gold Hunters," SFE, October 1, 1897.

"The Grand Cañon of the Colorado," CM, November, 1902.
"Alaska Land," SFDEB, October, 9, 1880.
"In the Heart of the California Alps," SM, July, 1880.
"Alaska Glaciers," SFDEB, September 23, 1879.
"Alaska Glaciers," SFDEB, September 23, 1879.
"Alaska Land," SFDEB, October 16, 1880.
"Wild Parks and Forest Reservations," AM, January, 1898.
"A Wind Storm in the Forests of the Yuba," SM, November, 1878.
"Alaska Land," SFDEB, October 9, 1880.
"A Great Storm," SFDEB, May 25, 1877.
"Wild Parks and Forest Reservations of the West," AM, January, 1898.
"Wild Parks and Forest Reservations of the West," AM, January, 1898.
"The National Parks and Forest Reservations," SCB, January, 1896.
"Summering in the Sierra," SFDEB, July 20, 1876.
"Winter Phenomena of the Yosemite Valley," PBSNH, 1873.
"Notes from Utah," SFDEB, June 14, 1877.
"The Forests of the Yosemite Park," AM, April, 1900.
"Exploration in the Great Tuolumne Cañon," OM, August, 1873.
"A Geologist's Winter Walk," OM, April, 1873.
"The Treasure's of the Yosemite," CM, August, 1890.
"A Geologist's Winter Walk," OM, April, 1873.
"Summering in the Sierra," SFDEB, November 17, 1875.
"Among the Birds of the Yosemite," AM, December, 1898.
"Among the Birds of the Yosemite," AM, December, 1898.
"Summering in the Sierra," SFDEB, August 12, 1876.
"Bee-Pastures of California," CM, July, 1882.
"Among the Animals of the Yosemite," AM, November, 1898.
"Among the Animals of the Yosemite," AM, November, 1898.
"A Letter from the Yosemite Valley," CR, March, 1905.
"The Yellowstone Park," SFDEB, October 27, 1885.
"Bee-Pastures of California," CM, July, 1882.
"A Rival of the Yosemite," CM, November, 1891.
"Alaska Coast Scenery," SFDEB, October 29, 1879.
"Modoc Memories," SFDEB, December 28, 1874.
"Yellowstone National Park," AM, April, 1898.
"A Geologist's Winter Walk," OM, April, 1873.
"Wild Parks and Forest Reservations," AM, January, 1898.
"The National Parks and Forest Reservations," SCB, January, 1896.
"Semi-Tropical California," SFDEB, September 7, 1877.
"Summering in the Sierra," SFDEB, July 20, 1876.
"A Letter from the Yosemite Valley," CR, March, 1905.

"Summering in the Sierra," SFDEB, August 13, 1875.
"A Letter from the Yosemite Valley," CR, March, 1905.
"Summering in the Sierra," SFDEB, August 13, 1875.
"Summering in the Sierra," SFDEB, August 13, 1875.
"The Glacier Meadows of the Sierra," SM, February, 1879.
"Among the Animals of the Yosemite," AM, November, 1898.
"In the San Gabriel," SFDEB, September 11, 1877.
"Mormon Lilies," SFDEB, July 19, 1877.
"Yosemite National Park," AM, August, 1899.
"The Yellowstone Park," SFDEB, October 27, 1885.
"The Treasures of the Yosemite," CM, August, 1890.
"Alaska Glaciers," SFDEB, September 23, 1879.
"Living Glaciers of California," HNMM, November, 1875.
"Summering in the Sierra," SFDEB, October 22, 1875.
"Snow Storm on Mount Shasta," HNMM, September, 1877.
"The Treasures of the Yosemite," CM, August, 1890.
"Summering in the Sierra," SFDEB, August 13, 1875.
"The Treasures of the Yosemite," CM, August, 1890.
"Three Adventures in the Yosemite," CM, March, 1912.
"Wild Parks and Forest Reservations," AM, January, 1898.
"Summering in the Sierra," SFDEB, August 3, 1875.
"A Sierra Flood Storm," SFDEBS, May 22, 1875.
"A Sierra Flood Storm," SFDEBS, May 22, 1875.
"In the Heart of the California Alps," SM, July, 1880.
"Wild Parks and Forest Reservations," AM, January, 1898.
"Summering in the Sierra," SFDEB, September 15, 1875.
"Snow Storm on Mount Shasta," HNMM, September, 1877.
"Summering in the Sierra," SFDEB, August 3, 1875.
"Three Adventures in the Yosemite," CM, March, 1912.
"God's First Temples," SDU, February 5, 1876.
"A Great Storm," SFDEB, May 25, 1877.
"Living Glaciers of California," HNMM, November, 1875.
"A Geologist's Winter Walk," OM, April, 1873.
"Living Glaciers of California," HNMM, November, 1875.

Bonnie Johanna Gisel is a naturalist, artist, nature writer, and historian who has written extensively about the life and work of John Muir. Presently she is at work on a book on John Muir and his life as a botanist. She is the author of the introduction to *John Muir: Family, Friends, and Adventures* and the author and editor of *Kindred & Related Spirits: The Letters of John Muir and Jeanne C. Carr*. She has published articles and lectured on John Muir and her own journeys in wilderness, including "A Song in Several Keys. Yosemite Journal," that appeared in *California Tour and Travel*. Bonnie is the curator at the Sierra Club's LeConte Memorial Lodge in Yosemite National Park, where she designs environmental education programs including the "Nature Journal," the Wilderness Quilt Project, Words for Wilderness Around the World, and Green Shoes.

www.ingramcontent.com/pod-product-compliance
Lightning Source LLC
Chambersburg PA
CBHW032123090426
42743CB00007B/436